# THE
# GOSPEL
# OF
# RELATIVITY

Books by Walter Starcke

THE DOUBLE THREAD
THE ULTIMATE REVOLUTION
HOMESICK FOR HEAVEN
THE GOSPEL OF RELATIVITY

# THE
# GOSPEL
# OF
# RELATIVITY

## WALTER STARCKE

Published by
GUADALUPE PRESS

Cover art and drawings by Ceanne Rusteen.
Mandalas by Jonathan Rainbow.

78 79 80 81 82 10 9 8 7 6 5 4

Library of Congress Cataloging in Publications Data

Starcke, Walter.
  The gospel of relativity.
  1. Christian life--1960-     I.  Title.
BV4501   248'4      88-072197      ISBN 0-929845-02-1

*I don't have to look far to see that all of us and every area of life are revealing dimensions of man and God in ways unique to this century. But four men in particular, each in his own way, have helped me understand what it means to love and express this new-found wholeness.*

*BODY*
*the paleontologist*
*Pierre Teilhard de Chardin,*
*who revealed how to love*
*matter or the earth . . .*

*MIND*
*the psychoanalyst Carl Jung,*
*who revealed how to love*
*the mind or consciousness . . .*

*SPIRIT*
*the mystic Joel Goldsmith,*
*who revealed how to love*
*God or the spirit in man . . .*

*AND*
*because relativity makes it possible*
*to integrate the three,*
*the mathematician Albert Einstein.*

*In this book there is a STORY:*


The Celebration of Life     

*and there is a TREASURE HUNT:*

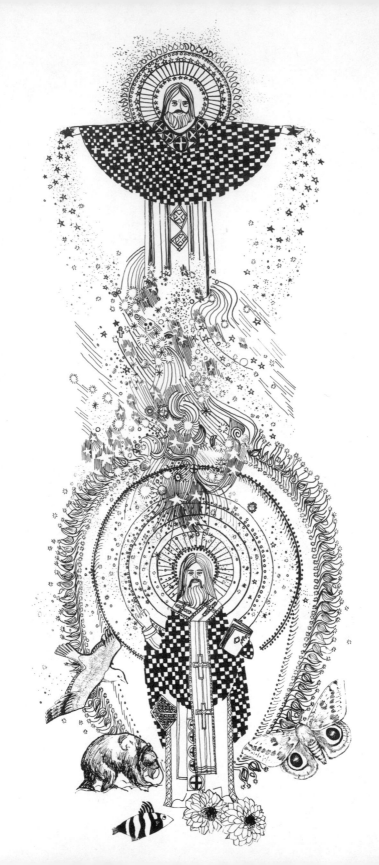

*Lulled by*
*stupefying illusions,*
*the world is asleep in the*
*cradle of infancy,*
*dreaming away the hours.*
*Material sense does not unfold*
*the facts of existence;*
*but spiritual sense lifts*
*human consciousness*
*into eternal*
*Truth.*

*—Mary Baker Eddy*

# THE
# CELEBRATION
# OF LIFE

The old man stepped out into the crisp morning-new air. Before walking to the top of the hill where the assembly hall had been built, he paused to enjoy a few deep breaths and let his eyes absorb the beauty around him. He marveled at the variety of green foliage, the awakening colors, and in particular, this day, the darting waltz of the brilliant butterflies. Perhaps he so greatly appreciated experiencing this now ordinary beauty because he was one of those who could remember when there were no more butterflies, when the world had been stripped of such glory, when the world came to its end.

In the past this old man would have been called a sage or a priest and the assembly hall a temple, but that was before mankind knew that the earth itself was the temple, that the celebration of life was the only ritual, that no one was superior to another and no one possessed—they shared. So the old man was just a storyteller on his way to share his story with those who came from miles around to hear.

The old man never tired of telling the story, because each telling added to the celebration. But beyond that, there was an important purpose for his telling it. His listeners were mainly the young who had been born in the new day. Most of them were reincarnations of those who had died at the end of the world. By hearing the story they would understand how they had arrived at their present freedom, where no sickness or pain existed, where poverty and inequality were inconceivable, and where consideration, patience, and love were as natural to man as breathing.

This old man wasn't the only one whose job and pleasure it was to tell the story. He happened to be in the center of one of the northern continents, but there were others all around the globe, on the tropical islands of the oceans, on the great plains, in the jungles, wherever there were those who wanted to hear the story as it had happened in their part of the world.

The assembly halls where the story was told were particularly personal and inspiring places. They were usually located on the crests of hills or wherever open sweeps of countryside could be experienced in order that the celebrants would not only be aware of each other but would feel and experience the wholeness and oneness of all being. It helped them appreciate the story all the more.

This assembly hall was built on a little hill at the end of a cultivated farm valley complete with a gurgling stream jumping with trout, a tiny village in the distance, and that feeling of alive stillness which vibrates from growing things. The hall radiated out from a big tree as a kind of focal point where the old man sat to tell his story. When he took his place, smiling faces greeted him with that recognition called love. He settled down, rested his back against the tree, and let his eyes drift silently across the valley. There was a long appreciative meditation; then he began.

"My story is about the last days of the world. You see, this planet earth was once called the world. Things were very different in those days. Mankind saw and understood the planet through a state of ignorance we now call the 'world view.' This 'world view' was a kind of blindness, a mistaken impression about the true nature of the earth and its inhabitants. As long as man was under the spell of this world view he acted in a strange and frightening manner, both in the way he mistreated his earth and in the way be mistreated his brothers. What we have come here today to hear is how he finally woke from his spell and found freedom in the end.

"Perhaps you'll understand those worldly men better if you realize that we ourselves didn't arrive where we are today in one jump. We evolved into our fullness, and that took thousands of years. First our bodies developed, then our minds, and finally our spirits blossomed so that we became what humans were meant to be. Evolution just hadn't reached its fullness until the end of the world, and when it did, the spell of subhuman man was broken. Before that time all man's problems, problems we don't have to-day, came from the fact that he was unable to keep himself in balance.

"Now, this imbalance didn't become dangerous until the mind grew too strong and began to dominate. The first dramatic illustration of the destructive nature of this imbalance happened in a place called Atlantis thousands of years before the end of the world itself. The Atlanteans brought forth a marvelous and almost perfect civilization, much as ours is today. They lived in cities of towering architectural beauty which seemed to complement nature, as clean and joyous to live in as anything we have, and there was nothing they were incapable of achieving. As the Atlanteans' mental powers grew, however, their technology developed the capacity to destroy life itself. The spiritual side hadn't evolved far enough to keep the mind in balance; so these Atlanteans lost the way and through their technology totally destroyed themselves.

"Fortunately, in those days the world did not react or function as one giant body, as it came to do in future years; so the Atlanteans destroyed only their own civilization and not the whole world. Nevertheless, the example of the Atlanteans should have tipped off mankind as to what was in store for the world if people didn't learn how to control the mind, but it didn't."

The old man stopped for a minute. His empathy told him that there were some who were perplexed over why the Atlanteans had let things get so drastically out of hand. Smiling with compassion he continued, "Don't forget, mankind was under a spell. Man was confused about who or what he was, like the prince who was hypnotized by the wizard into thinking he was a frog. At that time all men lived by what was called the first law of human nature. Actually it was the first law of subhuman nature, of man when he wasn't fully human, fully awake. That law tricked man into basing all his actions on something called 'fear.' Man could not come and go from his body as we can now; so he actually believed he was a destructible body, that if his body was destroyed he would cease to be. The first motive behind all his actions was to hang on to his body, thinking it was his true self. This mistaken belief was the wizard's spell that created the entire world view. It ceased only at the end of the world.

"Actually, it was a few thousand years after Atlantis until the first individual men evolved who broke the spell. In both the East and the West, evolution of individual beings advanced to the point where the first whole, unhypnotized men began to appear. In the West this new man appeared as one called Jesus the Christ. In the East one called Gautama the Buddha. These men were not only fully developed into what man could and should be, but they also knew themselves and just what it was to be fully human. Oh, yes, most assuredly, there were others who were born fully human of whom the public never knew, but these two were the first who were commonly recognized as having broken the spell.

"I say they were recognized, but that isn't quite true. People recognized that there was something very special about these men, but in general mankind stayed under the spell and didn't realize these men were telling them that they, too, could wake up and be free.

"Jesus and Gautama could do all the things we do today, could translate themselves into different vibrational levels of being, could turn into light or materialize in different places at will, could walk on water or through walls, but when they did these natural things their actions were called miracles. They tried in every way they knew to explain that they were not exceptions, that everyone could do as they did, but the people thought Jesus and Buddha were talking only about themselves. Nevertheless, at a subconscious level, mankind realized that these two were the flowering of the growth of man and worshiped them for it. The public didn't, however, heed their warnings that unless all followed their example man would destroy the world.

"Well, now," the old man continued with growing enthusiasm, "as the years passed, more and more, a few here and a few there, began to recognize their true selves and become human, and as they did, their spiritual energies added to the growing superspirit of all mankind.

"Finally, by the year 4667 of what was known as the Chinese calendar, or the twentieth century of the so-called Christian era, the world arrived at the same place Atlantis had, only this time there were two differences. This time the whole planet participated, and this time the power of spirit had evolved.

"Mankind was like a moth ready to emerge from its cocoon. But before a moth is kicked out of the cocoon it is unaware that it has grown from a grubby little worm into a thing of beauty. The moth doesn't realize that it has developed beautiful wings capable of lifting it freely into the infinite sunlight. Ignorant of its true being, the moth tries desperately to hang on to its hot, dark, and painful cocoon. That is, it hangs on until life forces it out into freedom. Now the big push began forcing man to wake up to his identity. Mankind, the sleeping prince, began to awaken—kissed by knowledge.

"You see, knowledge became self-multiplying. Because the rate of the growth of knowledge over the centuries had been slow, no one noticed that it grew in a kind of geometric progression. At first it was hundreds of years before accumulated knowledge doubled, but the gaps became shorter. For instance, recorded knowledge in books, laboratories, and such doubled between 1900 and 1950, then it took only ten years for it to double again. As more and more computers were speeding the process, the accumulation of knowledge doubled again in the next five years. The gap continued to narrow, so that in just a few more years man had access to infinite knowledge. From that time on, anything he could think he could do, any problem he could state he could solve.

"The new technology he created out of this infinite knowledge actually gave him access to limitless energy, but he didn't know how to use it because he was still under the spell of fear. Not realizing he could use his new sources of energy to free himself, he still clung to the age-old belief that he needed ninety percent of his personal energies to feed and clothe himself.

"Fathers left their homes each morning to go to work." The old man stopped for a second, frowned at the look of questioning on the faces of his listeners, broke into a smile, and said, "Oh, I forgot, you don't know what the word 'work' means. To work is to use one's energy and time doing something one doesn't want to do in order to obtain food and clothing. You see, in those days there was something called 'money.' Just as 'need' is the medium of exchange today, just as we go to the local warehouse for anything we need and simply take it—because in a planet without fear everything is shared and there is plenty for everyone—in

THE GOSPEL OF RELATIVITY

those days they had pieces of paper and metal called money with which they unlocked the doors of the warehouse. Most people went to work, put themselves through ordeals into which they could not take their whole selves—where they took their bodies and minds, but not their spirits—and in return for their pain, were given these keys to the warehouse.

"I know it is difficult to realize," the old man continued, "but in those confused days they actually imprisoned thirty or forty students in one classroom where all the teacher's energy was required just to keep them in their seats; fathers returned home after their needless hours of exhaustion with no energy left with which to love their families; and there was no one with enough energy to answer little children's questions, so the young grew up more or less unloved.

"If they had known how to let their spiritual natures control and direct the use of their limitless energy sources, they could have freed mankind as we have today. Now all parents are able to spend full time with their children, matching energy, loving, and experiencing together. Now we have the ideal condition of three or four students to a teacher, or guides as we call them, and now in all areas there is the energy and time for love, for answering each individual's problems, for eliminating loneliness and fear.

"The point is that by the twentieth century mankind had, for the first time in history, a technology which could have eliminated fear, that first law of human nature. Through his technology he could have guaranteed survival to everyone on the face of the earth, and by eliminating the law of human nature, everyone could have lived by the law of spiritual nature—love—as we do today. As strange as it may sound, mechanically man could have brought on the spiritual age.

"At any rate, visible cracks began to show in the world's life pattern. One of the first places the pattern broke was in relation to the young people. More and more of the young had the capacities to live as whole people similar to Jesus and Buddha, not just individually, but in mass. They confused the existing society by their looks and actions because, though the young themselves didn't realize it, they were potentially new-day people instilled with the ability to perform new-day professions. But society was still operating under the ninety-percent work law and not using its energies properly, so there was no place these young fit in. Many of them naturally refused work to which they were unable to bring their whole selves, and they spurned the keys to the warehouse, realizing the warehouse should be opened to all as needs dictated. Thousands upon thousands left the places of their birth and began to roam the farthest corners of the planet, subconsciously sensing that home was not a place but a state of mind, that the whole earth was home, and that all mankind was their family.

"The big issue which brought on the end of the world didn't come so much out of ignorance of the potential people had at their fingertips as it did out of the misuse of their new technology. They didn't blow themselves up as the Atlanteans did. They started poisoning themselves to death. In fact, they poisoned everything in sight—their water, their air, and their plant life as well.

"As soon as specialists in these various fields saw what was happening, they made predictions announcing that the end of life would come by the turn of the century unless immediate action was taken; however, at that time none of these specialists realized that because all areas were being poisoned, the effect each area had on the other would bring the end much sooner than expected.

"The first conclusive sign came with the ocean's death rattle. When man sprayed poison all over his earth trying to protect edible foods from insects, these poisons found their way into the ocean and slowed down the photosynthesis in marine plant life. Without this process, by which the sun's energy enters growing things, plant life in the ocean began to diminish. What's more, instead of exhausting themselves in the ocean these poisons, and one in particular with the innocent-sounding name of DDT, did not seem to wear out, even seemed to grow stronger as time passed.

"Of course the ocean and the air are just different aspects of the same elements, and what affects one affects the other; so when automobiles released great masses of poisonous carbons through their exhausts into the air, these poisons were not only breathed by man and plants; they eventually settled on the ground and were washed into the ocean. Or they floated in the air, changing the atmosphere to such a point that a heating effect was caused, which in turn affected the ocean. It was a vicious circle.

"Things were no better on land. The same process of breaking down the chain of life was taking place every-

where. Soon famine became widespread, first in the under-
developed nations and finally in the technologically advanced, but small, densely populated nations of Japan and
England. Up until this time, nations still operating under the
law of fear brought on the very things they feared by bickering and not using their aid as anything but a tool of war.

"You see, for many years there had been something
called the United Nations, where representatives of all nations met, but it had been little more than an international
gossip club. Now, however, it took on some real impor-
tance. When it was obvious that the ocean was dying, and
that crops were diminishing at a rapid rate, the small nations
gave up and threw themselves completely on the mercy of
the U.N. and the stronger nations.

"Finally there was utter chaos in America. Violence grew
out of hand as the habitability of America's great cities became impossible. Then in one hot month hundreds of thousands of corpses resulted from respiratory disease, and in
the wake of this national catastrophe the United States
turned over its authority to the U.N. It was followed by the
Soviet Union, Japan, and China.

"Actually, the final and conclusive issue which pushed
the world into placing itself under one supreme government
was the proof that the world was literally running out of
oxygen. It was shown that long before starvation would
overtake the world, the oxygen supply would be exhausted.
You see, most people had mistakenly thought that their
oxygen supply came from the plant life on the surface of the
earth, but only some fifteen percent came from the surface;
eighty-five percent came from the plankton and other plant
life in the ocean. As the ocean was almost dead, the supply
of new oxygen was almost eliminated. There was a consid-
erable quantity in the atmosphere, but unless the ocean was
returned to life it would only be a matter of time before all
the oxygen would be absorbed.

"When it became obvious that world catastrophe was
imminent, nations sent their most trusted and learned men
to the United Nations headquarters with full power to repre-
sent them. There was no bickering now. The General Assembly elected four men from the four corners of the world
to coordinate the general departments of administration and
to be the overall governing body.

"Survival was the one issue around which everything revolved. Complicated systems of communications were established at headquarters, linking all the universities, laboratories, weather stations, and monitoring satellites by interconnected computers. Experts in every field of science were sent to the U.N. headquarters to take up permanent residence. They worked in the U.N. laboratories and were in maximum person-to-person contact with each other and on constant closed-circuit television contact with their staffs and assistants around the world. Technology reached the epitome of expertise and efficiency.

"Having the records of all the factories of the world at hand, the computers soon showed that already as far back as 1969 the total production of DDT which had been manufactured was enough to kill the ocean, that as DDT did not disintegrate, it had only been a matter of time for it to be washed down from the land into the rivers and into the ocean. Even if the use of DDT had been stopped after 1969 it was already too late. Nineteen sixty-nine was the beginning of the end of the world.

"It was believed at first that either enough oxygen masks could be manufactured or enough bubble-enclosed cities could be built to sustain a portion of life on earth, but it was soon realized that if the lack of oxygen wouldn't finish off the earth, heat inversion would. Daily the indicators showed that the scientists were losing the battle. Orders went out to conserve oxygen in every way possible. All unnecessary travel, unnecessary production, and unnecessary use of oxygen were curtailed.

"The scientists worked feverishly searching for some way to reverse the death of the oceans and return them to a living state. Finally, after exploring thousands of master plans, one last plan emerged. The scientists formulated a new chemical, Xeron, which could neutralize DDT and the other poisons in the oceans. The Great Salt Lake was designated as a testing ground to try it out, and it was found that if enough of this new chemical was administered at just the right moment and in just the right quantity, a reaction could be induced which would indeed neutralize the poisons. But there was one catch: it took an enormous amount of Xeron to counteract the stupendous quantities of poisons that had been introduced into the world's oceans for so many years and that had been multiplying all this time. It was also discovered that when too little Xeron was administered, a reverse effect took place. The DDT not only dominated the chemical but in turn was stimulated by it into further virulence.

"Into the computers were fed all the facts relative to the sources of the various ingredients needed for the production of the antidote. Factory facilities presently existing which were suitable, and time and materials required to build more factories, were computed, as were access to various ingredients needed in Xeron, and transportation storage capacities. All of this was studied in relation to the increase of air pollution that would be brought on by production. The computations were checked and rechecked.

"As each day the ocean was dying at an increased rate, the computers showed the exact time when the maximum amount of Xeron could be produced and delivered to dumping stations around the world as against the danger of waiting for a guaranteed amount of chemical to do the job. Time was critical. If the ocean was allowed to continue as it was for very much longer, there would be no chance of stopping the DDT, and yet time was needed in order to produce enough antibody.

"The Council of Four heard the final report of the scientists. It was up to them to make the ultimate decision whether to go ahead or not. Their decision was all-important because if enough Xeron were to be produced, all other methods would have to be sacrificed for this one effort. If it didn't succeed, there would be no time left for another or different try. After long deliberation, they gave the order: Proceed!

"The entire population of the world was focused on this endeavor. Those who were not directly involved in the construction of factories, storage tanks, delivery systems, or in the manufacture of Xeron were either employed supplying food and medical aid and maintaining communication throughout the world or were ordered to stay quiet, use as little oxygen as possible, and wait.

"Everyone looked toward 'I Day'—Infusion Day. It took almost two years to mobilize the effort and produce the results. Each day thousands more were dying from a lack of food and oxygen. Finally 'I Day' came. Thousands of ships loaded with Xeron were stationed at given points around the world where the currents would best infuse the chemical through the oceans. Gigantic tanks had been built along coastlines in preparation for dumping the chemical into the coastal waters. Every ship and center was connected by satellite communication. On signal, at the exact moment the computers had dictated, the infusion took place. 'I Day' was over.

"The people of the world literally held their breath waiting for the results to register on the indicators. It was a time of quiet on the face of the earth. There was no visible sign of the great chemical war that was going on beneath of the surface of the oceans.

"These days of waiting were the first in several years when the Council of Four had been afforded any privacy. They each, as many others in the world, spent their time in silence and meditation.

"Then in a few days the monitoring stations' computers began to send in their reports. One by one, the story was the same. The attempt had failed. The poisons had triumphed. Within a very few years there would not be enough oxygen, food, or anything else for any life at all to survive on the face of the earth. The world was to become a gaseous, infernally hot, dead planet. Man had become the first life form not only powerful enough to alter its own evolution, but powerful enough to destroy the world."

The old man sighed in remembrance, then continued, "You might have thought that such news would send the world into panic, but it didn't. Actually, thousands had already taken their own lives in despair, and hope was already lost to many; so now there was only a kind of calm resignation, almost relief. Perhaps men had started too late, but in the end they had done everything they possibly could. Most importantly, many now felt stripped of their own responsibility, their minds were calm at last, and they could listen.

"It was in this attitude that the four leaders met at the appointed time. Each had heard the news in his own quarters, and, as had been previously agreed, when the final report was in they made their way to the central meeting room."

Once more the old man paused. He realized that his young listeners were caught up in the story because most of them now leaned forward or shifted their positions to make sure that they wouldn't miss a word. He continued, "In a way this meeting was one of the most significant moments in the history of man. All four of these leaders spoke almost as though they were thinking with one mind, a new universal mind, and their conclusions crystallized man's coming of age.

"Let me picture it for you if I can. The leaders came into the room and took their usual places around the polished conference table, but this time it was obvious things were different. Always in the past the table had been covered with piles of statistics and reports. Now it was empty. That emptiness was significant. It showed that all the decisions forged from the reports had been useless, that material or factual answers had failed. The looks that passed from one to the other showed that the significance of the empty table had not gone unnoticed.

"Yet, oddly enough, none of the leaders showed signs of despair or sadness. The first one to speak was the mathematician, economist, and production genius whose job it had been to channel the world's material and energy resources into the struggle for survival. He was a rugged-looking man, with clear, direct eyes and a friendly, though no-nonsense, approach. He started out explaining the sense of strange peace which had come to him and how he had had to abandon his usual proof-demanding approach in order to understand it, but that when he had, he came to some conclusions that made him believe man was on the edge of a new and total freedom.

"I'll try to put into words more or less what he said," the old man continued. "In making himself understood to the others, the mathematician explained, 'The clue which began to open my eyes to an avenue which could lead to freedom sounded almost too simpleminded to me when I started on that line, but the more I thought about it the more it checked out. Yesterday when I was taking a walk I looked up at the sun. My first thought was that perhaps we would be like the sun before long, a burning mass with no life. Then something inside my head said, "What makes you think there is no life on the sun?" and I answered, "The heat of the sun would make it impossible." After that it came to me that I've always believed there was no life on the sun because I've been too maddeningly literal. I've thought of life only as matter, as material.

" 'I've been working with forms of energy all my life. I've written papers explaining how all matter is energy expressed in form, even demonstrated that we have been able to split the atom because of this, but I was limiting myself. I didn't absorb the full meaning until now. Energy is the highest form of life, higher than the material forms or bodies we see with our eyes. We know that the sun is the greatest energy source in our solar system, and yet, somehow, we have felt that the sun is inferior to our earth, that we have life forms here but that the sun doesn't. If the sun is the highest energy source, couldn't it possibly contain the most highly evolved life forms, probably not just body forms as we conceive them but thought forms of pure energy, a kind of creative consciousness with awareness of life which isn't subject to material destruction? I have a feeling that every life form we have here and many more appear on the sun in forms that are not destructible in the ways we conceive.'

"By this time the mathematician wanted to pin down his reasoning in more practical terms, so he continued, 'I began to apply this line of reasoning to myself and my own body. First, I remembered that every cell in my body changes every seven years, that my cells regenerate and change form constantly. My body has materially changed every seven years, but I still feel a continuity of my self. When people say "hello" I don't number my different bodies. I don't say, "Me, number nine, says hello," though I would have had nine different bodies by now.

" 'Another thing, I've cut off pounds of hair and fingernails, peeled off skin through the years, and I haven't been upset by the loss. Even if my limbs were taken away, I'd still say, "I am here," not, "Two-thirds of me is here." Why? Because I am not body. I have a body, but I am not this body. Go ahead, save my body, but you wouldn't save me. And I won't be destroyed even if my body is.

" 'Now, it doesn't stop there. I am just as aware that my body is made up of atoms as I am that all matter is. The difference between my hand and this table is not a difference of basic substance; it's a difference of structure and density. This table is more dense and has a different inner structure, that's all. That means that the atoms in this table are vibrating at a different speed or density.

" 'As a mathematician I should have remembered Einstein's theory and realized that matter, when increased to the speed of light, theoretically becomes light; if all matter were lifted to the speed of light, it would become light and no longer be considered to be matter. But we would be wrong if we thought it stopped being matter; being light wouldn't really change it. It would still be matter, only seen in a higher form.

" 'If I can really identify myself with the highest form or use of energy, I will be able to translate myself into any form or level I wish. I will be able to convert energy into body or body into energy at will.'

"The mathematician paused as though talking to himself and said, 'What I am trying to say is that I've been so busy looking for material forms of energy that I haven't seen that science itself has been telling me I am a material body but I am also more than a material body, and when I really know and experience who I am, I will be able to manifest body at whatever level I wish. My very survival is dependent on my finding out who I am. What we are all facing is not a search for greater material powers, but rather we have been pushed into a tremendous worldwide identity crisis—a total identity emergency. If we can resolve that dilemma we will save the world.'

"The mathematician settled back and looked inquiringly into the faces of the three fellow leaders. There were nods of understanding and agreement. The next to continue the group's collective path to the answer was the representative from Asia, whose strength of intellect and integrity were etched across his dark face in denial of the frail slenderness of his body. His department was responsible for the inter-cooperation of governmental agencies, integration of minority groups, education, and all social needs. When he spoke it was in a gentle high voice flavored with a precise and clear pronunciation which seemed to melt the words together. He started by explaining that although he had spent most of his life in study around the world and in governmental services away from his home country, he was still rooted in the early Buddhist training. 'For years,' he explained, 'I have tried to approach my work impersonally, rationally, and as scientifically as possible in order to make sure that I was not caught up in a false sense of the world, but in the past few days I have come to see how limited the purely rational approach can be. I have found myself drawn into deeper and more penetrating meditations than it has been my fortune to experience for many, many years. In the depth of the silence I have experienced something close to the divine bliss I heard about as a child. I feel that for the first time I now see what Buddha meant when he said that life is illusory. I see that I have always accepted an illusory sense of who or what I am. At the very least I have misunderstood the relative nature of my self, and have not realized that I am both a man caught in the web of maya and a divine creature free and unlimited.

" 'However, my dear friends,' the gentle Asian continued, 'somewhere along the line a key has been missing, otherwise the messages of the mystics of the past would have freed us by now from this illusory sense of self. I tried to see what that key can be in the light of our new discoveries about the nature of man. It was only a scant hundred years ago when Dr. Freud in Vienna shocked the world by saying that man wasn't as simple as we had believed. He revealed that we were all of two minds, not just one, that we had a conscious mind and an unconscious one which apparently worked independently of each other. He went on to demonstrate that this unconscious mind could create organically sick bodies with very material illnesses that were not just psychosomatic. Then a few years later Dr. Carl Jung built on Freud's premise and lifted it into what I believe may be the very key we need to bring into fulfillment the knowledge of the mystics.

" 'Jung said that not only do we have a conscious mind and an unconscious, both of which have been built in our lifetime, but that we also are connected with a superconscious state that has existed for all time, a connection with all truth and knowledge—call it God if you will. Jung dignified man with divine consciousness and lifted him above being just a material body. In other words, he worked from the inside, from consciousness, to the outside form or body, demonstrating that we are primarily consciousness and that when we realize ourselves as being consciousness we can be free of our physical limitations.

" 'It stands to reason that if a misuse of our mind actually creates a malfunctioning body, then the proper use of our consciousness can create a harmoniously functioning body. If we could correct the misuse we could in turn learn not only how to create properly, but could begin to see that the creator is greater than creation, that somewhere we are more than our bodies, the bodies which our own consciousnesses have created.

" 'Perhaps Buddha too was saying that our illusory sense of life is the belief that we are body rather than consciousness. He said that the illusion of life was created out of our ignorance of our identity. Up until now we have been fighting the forms, have believed that survival lay in body rather than in consciousness. We have been struggling with the illusion rather than revealing the truth of being. Is that our mistake?

" 'In the Orient it is said that man lives by three kinds of food. The least important is the kind of food he puts into his mouth. He can survive for weeks without this kind of food. The next is food he breathes, without which he can survive for only seconds. But the most critical kind of food is the psychic impressions he takes into his mind. We have just about destroyed the first two foods, but perhaps our chance of survival lies in altering the food of consciousness.' "

The old man stopped using the high-pitched voice of the Asian representative and continued his account of the meeting: "As soon as the second leader stopped talking, all eyes at the table shifted to the renowned scientist who headed all the departments involving technology. There was something professorlike in this tall, dignified man that made you feel he could take the most complicated of ideas and express them in simple terms. His words went something like this, 'Last night my thoughts kept returning to the theories of the paleontologist-priest Pierre Teilhard de Chardin. Some years ago I was attracted to his scientistic theories because, though he was a priest, he believed that the answer lay in a further penetration into matter and the material world, not a rejection of the earth but rather an understanding of the relativity of its nature.

" 'I'd like to give you a perhaps oversimplified explanation of Teilhard's basic premise. He claimed that all growth takes place through the action of one fundamental principle. No matter if this growth principle results in the creation of an inanimate rock or a complex human being, the process is the same. All matter is made up of infinitesimally small particles. When enough of these elementary particles are drawn together they form atoms. Then when thousands of these atoms are symmetrically grouped they become molecules of carbon compounds. Next, when thousands of molecules are linked together, they become a cell, cells gathered together become tissue; collected tissue becomes body.

None of these stages happens by accident. The forms are compelled to change and become part of a new form. It is forced on them. It is forced on them because space becomes limited. If space isn't limited, nothing happens, but because a pressure of density is brought on by limited space the forms have to die or else become part of a larger life form. You might say that each stage represents an identity crisis.

" 'By "identity crisis" I mean that at each stage the life form has to cease being an isolated identity and find its identity as part of a new or larger being. It has to function as part of a larger identity or become isolated and be destroyed. In other words, Teilhard shows that all growth takes place by giving up a small identity for a new identity as part of a larger life form.

" 'Now, if our world had been an endless flat surface, space would not have been limited, and as more men appeared they could have kept their own independent idea of individuality and just spread out indefinitely. If this had been possible the problems of pollution, famine, and social conflict which we now face would not have come about. But the world is spherical; so as more humanity developed, the world became more and more compacted. Forces of compression due to the world's geometrical limitations have closed in on us, bringing on either destruction or a new sense of collective life. Teilhard called this process of growth "entropy." '

"The scientist hesitated for a second. With a pleased look of understanding he addressed his Asian colleague, 'I appreciated hearing just now that through your knowledge of Jung's theories you feel that the answer lies in our gaining a realization of the scope and power of consciousness because I feel those conclusions parallel Teilhard's. He believed that the next stage of evolution we are being pushed into is one involving a new understanding and relationship with consciousness.

" 'We know that everything down to the smallest particle has at least an elementary kind of consciousness. Just because an object is inanimate, that doesn't mean it doesn't contain consciousness, that it isn't alive. Everything, this table, this chair, is a living thing. We've all read reports proving that plants feel and respond to consciousness. And we have seen that as forms grow in complexity they grow in greater or more obvious consciousness. Matter becomes more conscious. You might say matter becomes more spiritualized. It seems to me, then, that matter can be converted into spirit.

" 'Actually, man proves that invisible spirit creates material forms. Man reflects, he has inner consciousness, and out of these invisible ideas or visions he creates. He even split the atom by this invisible consciousness. He also used this power to create the things that are now destroying the world; so maybe he can use that same power to save it.

" 'Something in me feels that as the world has become dense with greater consciousness the next stage of evolution we are being pushed into is the transcendence of consciousness over material and physical limitations. We are being pushed into identifying ourselves with consciousness rather than body. I guess we had to experience possible death as part of the entropy process forcing us into a larger sense of life, into a collective sense of life. Teilhard referred to this collective consciousness as though it was a kind of mass thinking envelope around the world. As I recall, Jung referred to it as the creation of a collective unconscious.

" 'I have no concrete idea how we can do it, but I feel that if we realize that we can become a kind of potential conversion machine able to convert matter into consciousness, we can also convert consciousness into matter. We will then not be confined to the old laws of matter but will be able to create a perfect and harmonious world out of our consciousness.'

"The scientist hesitated once more, but instead of continuing he turned to the last member of the group, the fatherly physician from America whose loving eyes, careworn face, and comfortable loose-fitting clothes more resembled an old-fashioned country doctor than the man upon whose shoulders the hopeless job of attempting to dispense medical aid to a dying world had fallen. It was almost as though all the others had made their comments first purposely, waiting for the physician whose loving spirit and personal manner had more than once lifted them when all hope seemed at an end.

"He spoke, 'Well, now, my friends, you don't know how happy you have made me. Listening to you made me feel newly born. You seemed to be speaking out of one voice. Each of you said what you had to say through the lens of your own profession and science, but there was one theme, and that theme reinforces a spark of hope that has come to me. Let me tell you of an experience I had this morning which gave rise to that hope.

" 'Though I have winked at God whenever I got a chance, there hasn't been much time for me really to sit down and talk to him for years. But these past few days have given me the opportunity to examine myself and my beliefs. Many of Christ's sayings, sayings I didn't even know I remembered from my childhood, came back to me. They took on new and far-reaching meanings. In a way I think I was pushed into hearing what he had to say for the first time. At any rate, this morning on my way to this meeting, when I passed the chapel below, I saw a service was in progress. I had a few minutes to spare, so I slipped in to listen and pray. It was then that I realized what service it was. It was the remembrance of Good Friday.

" 'As you know, Good Friday was the day Jesus was crucified. When I was a youth, I often wondered why it was called Good Friday—why not "bad Friday"? It certainly was a rough day for him. Now I know. On this day two thousand years ago, one individual man underwent the crucifixion of his body. He experienced the crucifixion of his own personal material sense and lived to tell of it. He hadn't wanted to undergo the agony of that experience. He said, "Let this cup pass from me," but evolution was forcing it upon him. If he had not been pushed into going through the experience, if he had managed to find some other way than the destruction of his body, he would not have proved that he was more than body, that he was a form of life eternal. He wouldn't have shown that he could lay down his body and pick it up.

" 'When I heard a minute ago that Teilhard referred to this process of evolution as entropy, I realized that Jesus' experience was one of entropy, of dying to be born. That was Jesus' great contribution to all of us. He, an individual man, was forced to die to his body sense in order to open the way for a new step in evolution for all mankind. But you know something—Jesus in his own words told us that we all had to die to have life eternal, that if we didn't die to thinking we were just bodies; we would not live eternally.

" 'Something else has just come to me. Since Jesus' day the same consciousness that was in him has grown universally to the point where, through this collective universal consciousness, I expect the world is now experiencing its mass Good Friday. Isn't it obvious that the day has now arrived when the world sense of materiality is being crucified?

" 'We certainly don't know of any material means to stop the end of the world. Right up until this very minute we have placed our faith and belief in material modes and means to save us, but they have failed. No matter how hard we have tried, we have been unable to overcome material powers by simply inventing still greater material powers. Instead of following Jesus' advice and rendering unto Caesar the things that are Caesar's, we have tried to out-Caesar Caesar.

" 'Maybe Jesus' words can show us how we can follow this universal Good Friday with an Easter resurrection for the earth. Jesus said, "My kingdom is not of this world." I always felt uncomfortable when I ran into that statement because I thought he was rejecting the earth and all the beautiful potential I saw in life, but now I see he meant that his kingdom was not in a materialistic, purely external concept of life. When he said, "I have overcome the world," he didn't say he had overcome the earth. He had overcome the false concept of earth. As a matter of fact, the Old Testament says, "The earth is the Lord's and the fullness thereof," meaning that the earth itself is in reality a heaven of truth, wholeness, and harmony.

" 'Because I had always interpreted Jesus' words as symbolic, I wasn't able to see that he quite literally means, "Destroy this body and in three days I will raise it up." He said, "I will raise *it* up," meaning: "I am not body. I have body, and I have the capacity to raise this body up any time I want." How? Not by fighting it, not by test tubes, not by adding more flesh, but through consciousness, by attaining an awareness of my true being, by knowing who I am.

" 'Jesus explained what that withinness was. He said, "I am the way, the truth, and the life." "I." He didn't mean that he, Jesus, was the "I" alone, but that each one of us could say "I," that each one of us has a unity with life eternal and that this unity is "I." He said, "I am the light," and though we have thought he was speaking philosophically, my friend here just told us that it is a scientific fact. Jesus, through consciousness, could raise himself to the speed of light and transcend material law. Through consciousness he became free of physical death. He could not be killed; he could lay down his body and take it up.

" 'We can lay down our bodies, too, and take them up if we can attain Christ-consciousness. That consciousness is the realization of who we are. It is simply the resolution of the universal identity crisis we are facing. Our survival depends entirely on whether we can transcend the centuries of spiritual sleep and ignorance before it is too late.

" 'If we fight the words, if we believe it is impossible for us to do what Jesus did, that Jesus was an exception, then there is no way to raise up our bodies. But if we utilize all our technology along with our spiritual awareness and stop just giving the Christian example lip service, we can lift enough of mankind into the realization that resurrection is not symbolic, but an *actuality*. We may have time between this universal Good Friday and the few months that life can be sustained in the old awareness to bring a universal Easter and with it a freedom over all material law.'

"A great rush of excitement swept the room. Everyone spoke at once, but it was as though one mind was speaking, with each finishing the sentences of the other."

The excitement among the listeners in the meeting hall where the old man was telling the story matched the excitement he had been describing in the story. His listeners were simultaneously eager to show their delight in seeing how the new awareness had been arrived at and anxious for the old man to continue so they could hear what happened next. He leaned forward and went on with his explanation: "The leaders spent hours crystallizing their concepts into central points. First they realized that since only a few had been able to rise to the level of Jesus or Buddha in the past, it was necessary now that great numbers do so in order for the universal consciousness to be affected. Then they realized that there was reason to hope this could be done now for the first time.

"In the past, spiritual illumination had not been a necessity, so most people just played at it; its becoming a necessity had opened up inner capacities, making it more easily attained now. Then, too, the world had arrived at the place where opposing dualities such as the conflict between Eastern and Western thought, or the conflict between religion and science, had been outgrown, and now all sides contributed to a new wholeness.

"Overnight the entire scientific and technological know-how of the world was directed toward this goal of building the new universal consciousness. All the beliefs and theories of all the world's religions were fed into computers, cross-referenced, calibrated, and defined. Temples in China containing manuscripts which few had ever seen, because it was said that man could not read them and stay sane, were entered and their secrets fed into the computers. The lamas who had remained hidden in Tibet came out of seclusion and were flown to headquarters for consultation and meditation. Various groups of students were chosen for their unique abilities. Some were flown to sacred mountains or holy places for special meditation and instruction, while others worked on specific areas of spiritual practice.

"The most successful techniques of spiritual healing methods were studied. Christian Science principles were illuminated by the most successful practitioners. The facilities at the headquarters of the Unity Church, where healing techniques had been practiced for years, became the center for metaphysical teachers, with representatives of Theosophy, the Arcane School, Religious Science, and various other metaphysical teachers working around the clock.

"The thousands of readings of the psychic Edgar Cayce were pored over for clues. His followers and the top parapsychologists were given unlimited financial and technical assistance in order to test his principles.

"The archives of the Catholic Church were explored, seeking early Christian manuscripts which might reveal light on the principles of transmutation practiced by the early church which still demonstrated the secrets of spiritual healing.

"Students of Yoga made enormous progress in setting aside many of the physical laws by demonstrating that each bodily function could be brought back to conscious awareness and could be consciously controlled.

"Zen masters demonstrated unbelievable powers to direct soul-awakening energy through meditation. Under their direction many students attained depths of meditation in a matter of weeks that had been attained only by years of concentration in the past.

"Heretofore esoteric Rosicrucian texts revealed the secrets of the pyramids, and the Book of Urantia was carefully studied in order to enlist aid from the spiritual hierarchy.

"Simultaneously, the general public was totally dedicated to the study of religion and the spiritual life. No longer was religion the superstitious chess game it had always been. It wasn't uncommon to see staid dowagers assuming the lotus position to meditate, or truck drivers stopping by the highway for their quiet time. Fasting and other spiritual aids were practiced regularly among the police and government officials. The daily newspaper headlines announced new techniques of spiritual healing.

"Hourly reports poured in to the United Nations central. Successes were computed and failures noted. All indicators were watched carefully. Avenues which showed little progress were discontinued, while attempts were made to combine successful techniques of one teaching with successful areas of other teachings. Certain masters who demonstrated powers of lifting consciousness were brought together with the most advanced students.

"But it was soon obvious that time was running out. A few years earlier no one would have believed how many laws could be set aside and how much freedom could be attained, but still there were too many failures covering large areas, and progress was too slow.

"Then the computers revealed an interesting fact. With few exceptions, all people over a certain age were progressing more slowly than those of younger years. At least it became apparent that there was a far greater degree of progress among certain of the young. Older people seemed able to generate enormous spiritual power through meditation and were doubtlessly helping build the new envelope of consciousness, but individually they were not vibrating at a level that would transcend matter and convert it into spirit.

"The answer to the problem of the older generations was revealed. Those who had been conditioned before the atom had been split were not able to rise far enough in consciousness. They had been so conditioned by materiality that the jump was too great. Before the atom was split, everything was seen as having a visible explanation. Although man speculated on the spiritual, with few exceptions the material fact before him was all he could really accept. He was totally conditioned by material appearances: speed came from the visible muscles in the horse's legs, light from the burning of visible wax, and so forth. But after the splitting of the atom the invisibles were put on an equal footing with the visibles, and the young were conditioned to accept invisibles easily. For them, the jump in consciousness was not as great.

"It was not only reported that the young were able to

progress more quickly than the old, but it was seen that the group of young who responded most quickly of all were many of the same young who had been rejected by society a few years before because of their differences of opinion, hair, dress, and refusal to work in the established systems. The same consciousness which made it impossible for them to fit in with society was the very thing that made it possible for them to respond to the new.

"Once more the computers were consulted. They revealed that scattered around the world were just enough of these unconditioned young with the basic capacity of attaining the new consciousness. If all these were helped into the new awareness, were able to generate the energy of the higher consciousness, the awakening could take place and there would be a new lease on life for the earth. All agencies now centered on helping the young and their teachers. When the older people knew they would not be able to attain personal freedom individually, they selflessly added to the power of love or spirit in every way they could by prayer, meditation, and encouraging the young.

"Eventually more and more of the young began actually to attain the realization that they were consciousness rather than body. Effects began to lose power over them. Medicine no longer worked on them, proving that they were going beyond material cause.

"It became obvious that there was a direct ratio between the fear in man and the power inherent in material things, that in direct ratio as man was able to rise beyond the consciousness of fear, the material destruction ceased. Whereas there was no material force which could stem the power of DDT, now that the fear of it was lessening, DDT was no longer able to destroy.

"Of course, this lessening of fear did not happen overnight, nor were all people able to rise above fear. What really took place was a change in consciousness. It wasn't that the earth died. What died was the "this world" spell, and when that ignorance left, the power of destruction left as well and the earth became Itself. It had been the poison in the old consciousness that had been poisoning the earth.

"Those who were not able to become free, who were not able to eliminate the poison of "this world" consciousness from their minds, succumbed. The older generations were mainly the ones who had been so indoctrinated that they were unable to attain full freedom, but as the old were dying, more and more of the young were resolving their body sense and were finding out that they were no longer subject to the laws of matter or fear.

"Aging beyond maturity stopped. As now, people reached their maturity and stayed there without any further deterioration. Finally more and more of the young attained the ability to come and go from their bodies. The ignorance and hypnotism of materiality was ending.

"Now, when anyone needed an answer he knew that he could turn within, lift his consciousness into the impersonal universal source of all knowledge, and return with whatever knowledge he needed. He knew that since he was connected with all others through the collective unconscious he could contact anyone he needed by reaching out spiritually to that person through this divine link.

"When it was understood that everything in the world of effect, anything that could be seen or touched, was the result of consciousness expressed in form, it was a simple matter to change the forms into harmonious and perfect oneness simply by changing consciousness. Automobiles operated without any destructive side effects because poisons were eliminated through consciousness. Everything worked in harmony, and because it was realized that infinite supply was an activity of consciousness, all lack disappeared.

"The naturally harmonious flow of nature began to resume. The earth began to look more beautiful than it ever had when it was the world. It had similar trees, similar flowers, the same star-filled nights with the same lovely fireflies, but now it was pure consciousness expressing itself. People no longer stopped at a superficial or face value impression of life but were aware of the invisible consciousness as the source of life. The only thing that had ended was the misconception of what life really was. Now everyone knew that there was only One. Because everyone was constantly aware of this oneness, all life and all being responded in perfect harmony.

"This beauty and perfection came about simply because the identity dilemma had been resolved. Now mankind knew he was consciousness or spirit rather than just material form. Being infinite, he knew he had an individual identity made up of body, mind, and spirit, but having gained the

capacity to see himself in a relative fashion, he could celebrate all of life and self and was free to operate at any level.

"The false sense of life burned off by the light of truth
lifted like a fog. The new earth appeared right in the place
where the old world of plague and famine had once been,
and living became a continuous celebration of life."

When the old man finished, the wave of empathy sur-
rounding him was stronger than ever. The smiling eyes of his
listeners told him that none had become frightened by his
story, nor had any suffered from the echo of aches left over
from their past incarnations; rather, they all glowed with
greater appreciation for the present.

"Now," the old man went on as he rose from his seat,
"those of you who would like to get a feel of what it was
to be one of those awakening people, come with me to the
museum, and I will show you some of the relics from the age
of religion, some of the primitive tools man used in attaining
his freedom."

In the museum the old man paused before a shelf of
manuscripts. "Here are some of the teachings assembled by
those who were working with the young at the end of the
world. You will be amazed at these teachers' clumsiness,
how close to the truth they were, but how unable they were
to voice it. You must realize that these were primitive men
who didn't really know who they were, but who somehow
had the clue that the secret lay in finding their right identification."

He stopped before a particular shelf and picked up a
battered old manuscript. He held it lovingly and said, "This
book was written during the 1970's, not long before the end
of the world. It was written by one of those who had a great
struggle of his own trying to face the identity crisis. He was
too old to actually make it across in the same body, but his
own search revealed some keys which helped others. He
was a bridge.

"I submit this book because it is valuable to see how the
truths which eventually led to the freedom of mankind were
voiced at that time, though stumblingly. But, you see, I am
partial. I was one of the young who survived. This book was
written by one of my teachers, and I am grateful because
although he was just barely on the edge of understanding,
he helped me find out who I am. Here is his book."

# THE MAP

I write religious books not because I am spiritual—just the opposite. All my life I've been struggling to learn what it is to be spiritual. If I were "there," I would not have had to find the way step by step. Naturally, I feel that I've made some progress; in fact, at times I've broken through into absolute consciousness, and I've reason to believe that those experiences of pure consciousness can be broadened into total realization. But when that time comes, I'll no longer be around to talk about it and certainly won't be writing books.

In the meantime there is a specific reason for my writing this one. I know, firsthand, how agonizing it is to have searched high and low finding truths from all kinds of religions and teachers only to end up feeling a failure because I hadn't made my own life work as I wanted, hadn't been able to put all the pieces together in some kind of order that fit me individually. I know what it is to have evolved to the point where I could no longer lean on a guru or seek new religions but had to find the guru or god source within myself. I know what it is to have made the mistake of turning my back on my human self, trying to be spiritual instead of realizing that things are not either/or. I know what it is to arrive at the lonely place where I just wanted to belong to the family of man and not identify with any particular group or type by my appearance or actions.

Finally, I know what it is to experience a devastating dark night of the soul where my lifetime of searching seemed a total loss, where I felt cut off from God or anything I had sought, where there was no hope, no future, nothing but empty blankness—only then to be rewarded by the final pieces of the puzzle of life, the realizations that made everything fall into place. That's why I must write this book.

Actually, it is not really a book at all, it's a MAP—a word map, a treasure map if you will. It holds out the promise that if all the ideas, all the clues, are understood and experienced, not only will frustrations and dark nights disappear but a divine treasure, the greatest of all, will be revealed in the end.

In searching for the treasure, I, like a lot of you, have studied many maps, Occidental and Oriental, new and old. But in the process I found a big stumbling block which has kept many sincere searchers from ever arriving at the treasure. Each of the maps could have led them to a successful experience had its clues been followed, but in their zeal often the searchers got sidetracked by trying to mix too many clues from too many different maps. Each of the clues was true in the context of its own map, but it's a mistake to believe that clues interchange and should all be shoved into one map. We come much closer to making a successful journey if we choose one map at a time, find a guide who knows that particular route, put clues to other maps out of our mind, and stick to the chosen map.

Since I am writing in the English language, most of those who find this map will come out of Western cultures. The most important of the Western maps is the Christian Bible, so I will take the clues set forth in the Christian message, add a few individual interpretations that I feel are vitally important keys, and aim at the treasure Jesus said was our birthright.

The uniqueness of this particular interpretation lies, perhaps, more on where the emphasis is placed than on the clues themselves—but that subtlety can make all the difference between total success and total failure.

But now, if Christian scriptures bother you because they have been mauled by misinterpretation or if you have been blinded by the hypocritical concepts of God, love, and truth so often voiced in the name of Christianity, perhaps you can't follow a map outlined in scriptures and this is not the trip for you. If, on the other hand, you think it is time you shook off misconceptions and got a new line on the map Jesus was trying to reveal, then you may be way ahead of those who come to this journey certain that they already know the correct interpretation.

To tell the truth, no one is free of misinterpreted truth until he sees truth correctly interpreted. Damping misconceptions down in the unconscious just leaves them festering there. I believe that those of us who were born in Christian cultures were not born here by accident and are never fully reconciled to our roots until we appreciate the message of our background free from distortions.

So, once more, if you are sure you know the true direction, if you are wedded to the clues you have already discovered, or if you are unable to wash out your brain in order to receive a fresh interpretation, you had better not try to make this particular trip. Except you come as a child, with the open willingness to play the game by the rules here set down—stop. You are only going to cheat yourself if you think: I'll look into this book, but I already know the true way; I'll just take what I approve of and reject the rest. You might find yourself caught in the middle, unable to go forward and unable to return to past beliefs.

Then, those who want to continue, let us be in accord about the reasons for the journey and what the treasure is. Unless we are in complete agreement we can't possibly keep our focus on the goal. The limitations of word and mind make it impossible. So, as I see it, what has caused us to take the journey, what we hope to achieve, is this: there are some of us who believe from the signs of the times and the reports of the mystics that material life as we know it on earth is not only becoming increasingly difficult to cope with but may even cease to exist before too many years. We believe that those who will overcome the world, who will survive, will be those who have managed to break the brainwashing which has hypnotized them into believing that they are material beings—not spiritual beings who have material bodies. We believe the guides from the past who have said that it is possible to overcome this erroneous sense of self and, by attaining an awareness of true identity, have life eternal. The treasure at the end of the search is the ability to break the laws of matter which bind us to this false sense of self and therefore attain eternal freedom, joy, harmony, and abundance—just barely dreamed of in our present state.

If those premises are accepted, if something right down to the depths of your being says, "Yes. That is the purpose of life. I must sell all to buy that pearl of great price, there is no more wonderful art than the creation of my self. I will not turn back. I can't turn back. I will take my whole self into this search, and I will give my guide all the help I can by trying in every way to hear his clues freed of past judgments,'' there is a chance we, together, for it will take all our energies, can cross the jungles of ignorance and reach the treasure.

The next question you should ask yourself is: *What guide is best for me?* Your guide should be one who has made the trip himself, at least come close enough to the treasure to have caught a momentary vision of it. But just because a guide has seen the treasure doesn't necessarily make him the best one for you. Your guide must be able to speak your language—not just word language, but the language of being. You must feel that your guide is part of your spiritual family, perhaps even a guide with whom you associated in a past life.

Another thing to realize is that the best guide isn't necessarily one who has experienced the treasure the greatest number of times or with the greatest intensity. Such a guide might set too strong a pace for you to follow, might give unrecognizable clues beyond your present reach. Perhaps a younger or less sure guide, one more like you yourself, but one who has made the trip at least once, would let you share in the discovery and share in drawing a new map, a map which is really partly your own. Then you, too, might be better able to help guide others in the future—and that would be the best guide for you.

If you are already under the direction of a guide, ask yourself if he is the right one for you. There are many guides, and there's no harm in shopping around until you are led from within to your particular one. It is possible to have several guides in a single lifetime, but it is next to impossible to listen to several guides at the same time without getting confused. Believe me, no two guides are exactly alike. It's an impossibility. So don't fear that you will not find the right one, don't jump on bandwagons or be tricked by publicity. Your own inner guide will direct you to your outer guide. Just listen.

One of the best ways to know if a guide is truly a designated teacher is to find out if he claims his map is complete or final. No map is. No matter how many times a guide makes a trip, he finds new clues among the familiar signposts. A true guide rediscovers the treasure anew each time. He couldn't make the trip over and over if he didn't need to reexperience the treasure himself.

Now, I am the guide on this particular expedition. I don't claim to be a fully awake guide. I'm not. I have experienced the treasure, and I have an insatiable desire to experience it over and over until the path is so clear and worn that I never lose sight of it. Don't feel bad if I am not the guide for you. I am not interested in taking searchers away from any other guide, and I certainly do not want to attempt to guide large numbers to the treasure. The larger the group, the more difficult the trip.

As a guide I face a further problem by writing the map down as a book. If you and I were together in person you could stop me and ask for clarification when I gave you obscure clues. I could see from your eyes when you were not understanding. But I have no way in a book to know if wrong turns have been made, if I have not given clear clues. It demands an extra patience, love, and inner faith for both of us to make the trip with this handicap. Perhaps we can make it in person someday, but for now we face this limitation.

We face another limitation which is almost impossible to transcend. We want to have a spiritual experience, but we are using words. Words can't be spiritual; they are mental.

You see, the spiritual sense is a different sense from the mental one, and no sense can be translated into terms of another—none. For instance, try explaining color to a blind man. It's impossible. You can't say, "Red is like this apple feels." No, each sense must be experienced on its own. So as we go along, although we are using mental words, we have to resist the temptation to get intellectual. We must hang loose and let ourselves experience the spirit of what is being said rather than the words themselves.

Finally, I will doubtlessly repeat some of the clues I have revealed in my other trips, my other books, *This Double Thread* and *The Ultimate Revolution,* because they are basic to my particular path to the treasure. Of course many of these directions have come from other guides. I'm always delighted when I find that things I thought were original were included in maps drawn by others years before I was even around. It makes me know I have tuned into the master map.

One guide in particular, Joel Goldsmith, was most influential in guiding me for many years, and those of you who have studied his map will recognize many similar signposts. Of course he, in turn, got many of his clues from a whole chain of guides leading back to Jesus, who in turn received revelations handed down from the beginning of time.

I'm sure that as the mystics of the past approached the treasure, they shared many of the same clues and learned from each other—that, for instance, the Buddha and the Christ walked hand in hand.

Before we start the journey, there is one definite prerequi-
site or ability which each of those who wish to join the
expedition must have in order to experience the clues un-
compromisingly. Without this talent, success is impossible.
If you do not qualify I suggest that you postpone beginning
until you have developed some strength and facility in this
area. That requirement is the knowledge of the purpose of
MEDITATION and the ability to meditate.

Most people fail in following maps because they have not
realized that merely understanding clues with their minds is
not enough. Unless each clue is experienced, and experienced in proper order, the whole trip is sidetracked.

Most of you who have even picked up this book are
probably familiar with meditation, even meditation as a way
of life, or you would not have been directed this far; so you
already understand why meditation is a requirement.

Technically, this is what meditation accomplishes. We are
starting this journey with our conscious mind. That conscious mind is like the one-eighth of the iceberg which appears above the surface of the ocean. The seven-eighths not
apparent to the naked eye is the subconscious. Beyond the
subconscious is the collective unconscious, the noosphere,
universal consciousness, or the total Godhead. This collective unconscious is like the ocean in which all the icebergs
float. This ocean is not only the means of communication
between all the individual icebergs, but it is the collection of
total truth to which we, as individual icebergs, have access.
Through meditation we contact that total truth, we transcend our finite limitations, and we communicate with each
other.

Meditation is simply the name we put on whatever means
we use in order to turn within and go from our conscious,
through our unconscious, into the experience of pure truth
or God. There are numerous techniques for meditation, and
unfortunately many people get the techniques mixed up
with the purpose. People often get so tied up in the techniques that they never attain the goal of going beyond their
limitations.

Meditating is like throwing a pot. When a potter sits down
to throw, he takes the clay into his hands. His first goal is
to get the clay centered. This is absolutely necessary before
he can even begin to lift it up into a work of art.

To center the clay is to condense it, press it into shape,

mold it, unify it, until it is all pulled together, until it revolves between the hands of the potter without wobbling, without even vibrating, as though it is still, despite the whirling turns of the wheel.

Sometimes as he is pressing the clay, concentrating on it, holding it and directing it toward the center, the potter must sort of pull the clay up into a mound and press it down again into the centered ball in order to get all the bubbles out, eliminate the impurities, and bring it to that smooth silence. But finally when all is quiet, when the clay feels serene as it turns between his hands, the potter knows the time has come to direct the clay into a thing of beauty.

When the clay is centered and the potter is ready to see what the clay has to reveal, it is like the moment in meditation where one asks, "Now, speak, Father, thy servant's ears are open to listen." And the truth is experienced in form.

That is what we do with our selves in meditation. We sit down in our physical or intellectual sense in order first to be centered and then to experience the revelation of truth. Anything that helps us become centered is a technique of meditation. We may even simply find that central point of self within us and concentrate on bringing our whole self into harmony and oneness with it until we feel ourselves smoothly revolving between the hands of spirit. We may find that in the centering process there are times when we are trying too hard and must, as the potter lifts up the clay, get up and walk around, pick some flowers, sing a song, make some music, and then return to the centering process until we feel we have gone into the silence—the world is turning but we are still and serene at the center.

But we don't stop there. The next step is to listen to the truth or the clue until it is lifted through the unconscious into the universal and is experienced; then it has become part of our individual consciousness and can be intellectually understood even at the personal conscious level.

Meditation is the avenue which takes us from individual hearing and reading into the source of eternal being and experiencing. For some it can be achieved quickly, and for others more time is necessary, but for everyone it is the only way the map of spirit is followed to the treasure.

Whenever a clue in this map strikes a chord, stop, center it, and listen to whatever personal creation or revelation you can add to the clue (we are all building the ultimate map),

but most assuredly, stop and meditate when you are instructed to.

In the course of our journey, as your guide, I will ask that
you close the map, turn within, and sit in silence until you
feel you have not only thought about the clue but have
experienced the truth of it. If you can't feel an inner click,
a sense of inner realization, then I suggest you read the
preceding section over again and see if you can't receive
some light on the clue.

Throughout the map you'll see some designs, mandalas,
and figures. These are the signals to meditate. When they
appear, put the book aside for a moment and see if you can
experience the clue you have just been given.

Let me suggest at this junction that you make your own
personal log and journal of the trip. Get a blank composition
book and have it by your side. Whenever in your meditation
you have contacted the center and received additional revelations on the clue, jot them down in your own map or diary
of the trip. Perhaps we can share them when the trip is over,
and add to the master map. At any rate, I do know that what
you put in your book will return to you with fantastic freeing
power if and when you grow weary of the journey or if in
the future you forget your way once more.

It is also necessary to keep your log secret and sacred.
Secret in that you keep it hidden from unprepared eyes,
from those who have not made the journey. Make the log
cryptic, and express the revelations in as short a form as
possible, a brevity which would confuse unprepared eyes.
Then the log should be kept sacred in that you should not
put idle thoughts in it but only insert those experiences or
ideas that come to you from within, with power. If you felt
a "click" or an experience along with the idea, it most likely
has come from spirit and is sacred enough for your spiritual
journal.

My previous maps, as well as this one, have come by bits
and pieces over the years from the clues I have put in my
logs of past journeys. Keep a log, and at the end you'll have
your own unique map.

Now, stop reading. Feel what you have heard so far. Ask
yourself if you must make the journey or not. If you don't
have to make it, it's probably better that you don't. Ask
yourself if you are as ready to bring your whole self into the
journey as I am in attempting to reveal myself by outlining

the map. Ask yourself if you are ready to read between the lines and experience rather than argue. And, finally, ask yourself if you are prepared to make the whole journey, because partial trips, dipping here, tasting there, will not succeed. Meditate, center, and if this is not your trip just wish us well, find your own trip, and perhaps we'll arrive together joyously at the treasure.

# THE
# RELATIVE
# PERFECTION

Truth is a gift of God. You don't have to earn it by unlocking involved theologies. Searching for mind-bending secrets bogs you down in a jungle of religious dead ends. Wise men have always known the best way to hide a secret anyway was to stick it right under people's noses and make it obvious. '

When, after years of frantic searching, I finally got still enough to become aware of the most obvious clue of all, the whole path opened like magic. It came to me on top of Haleakala, the volcano on the island of Maui. Sitting at the rim of the crater meditating, blank and unthinking, I was handed the gift of this clue. Like a tape recorder in my head the inner voice said, "Why do you think Jesus gave us TWO commandments, not just one? He said, 'Love the Lord thy God with all thy heart, and with all thy soul, and with all thy mind. This is the first commandment. And a second is like unto it, thou shalt love thy neighbor as thy self. On these two commandments hang all the law' " (Matt. 22:37–40).

Jesus didn't lay an ABSOLUTE trip on us. He was trying to tell us that our whole problem was simply an identity crisis which would be resolved when we learned how to identify and love the infinite invisible nature of life on the one hand, and love the finite, unabsolute nature of the visible self and world on the other hand. Simply, that things are not either/or. Never. We are both man of earth and man of God. We must be aware of both sides and how they relate to each other in order to realize that the two are really one.

It's a paradox, but the way we arrive at the realization that everything is ONE is by approaching from two sides. The secret Jesus gave us is that in order to experience a true nonduality we first have to accept what appears as a duality —two commandments.

I was surprised to be given this clue in terms of Christian scriptures because up until this time the Bible made no sense to me. But when I saw that whenever Jesus talked about "righteous judgment" he was talking about right identification, that whenever he talked about love he was talking about seeing true identity, the Bible opened up. I saw that the entire Bible was nothing more than an explanation of the identity dilemma which creates the entire human scene, and that every principle Jesus gave was about how to solve the dilemma so that we could be free.

Whenever you read the Bible see if everything, in one way or another, doesn't relate to either the cause or the solution of the identity crisis.

I know it sounds too simple to believe, but total freedom, eternal life, complete fulfillment, and actual transcendence over material limitations are attained by one thing and one thing alone—by resolving the identity crisis. When you really know who or what your human identity is, and who or what your God identity is, you are free. This is done when you consciously realize how to comprehend the *relative* nature of the two commandments.

Just the other day I was discussing this double-thread approach with an old friend. When I complained about some of the difficulties in making myself understood, my friend hopped on me for even trying. He said that admitting for one second that there was a material level would tear me to pieces. I couldn't agree. If we were not to admit the finite or neighbor level, why did Jesus give us two commandments? Why didn't he just say, "Love God," and leave it at that? He didn't because he knew that all those who call themselves absolutists, who refuse to admit that there is a human scene, are kidding themselves when they say they never see the flesh or finite side. To really be an absolutist you have to be able to see all sides of absolutely everything. The mystic who rejects the material world, saying it is illusion, creates a dualism composed of reality and illusion. He is dualistic, not absolute.

Certainly absolutes exist; no one is denying that nor denying that it is necessary to comprehend them in order eventually to experience them. But it is a stumbling block when one expects to find absolutes at the finite, or less than absolute, level. By knowing the absolutes, and then by knowing the finite, it is possible to see how they relate. It is possible to see how the finite expresses the absolute in less than absolute terms, and in that double-thread way lies the answer.

Keep in mind, however, that when I talk about the double thread I am *not* talking about two threads. I am talking about one truth, one thread, made up of two strands. One strand is the absolute spiritual identity, and one is the less-than-absolute human identity. The answer lies in not rejecting either of these strands, but in combining them through right identification until freedom is attained.

You might wonder why man hasn't done this in the past if it is so simple. But there's a reason. It takes the ability to "double think," and man has only now evolved to the point where he can consciously do that.

Up until now man hasn't been able to think of two things at once, not really. If he sees the front of a house, he can't see the back. When he goes around to the back, he loses sight of the front. But now we are developing a new sense —the ability to sense or hold the picture of the front in our consciousness while we actually look at the back in such a way that we retain a whole picture. It's sort of like having the ability to superimpose one on the other without confusing either. And it's the key to thinking relatively.

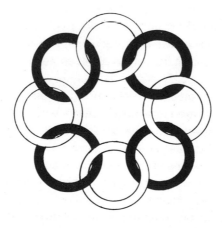

*Take time to absorb this. Close your eyes if you
need. First think and then feel. Feel the double
nature of your own being. Feel the two sides into
oneness. Realize that IN ORDER TO EXPERIENCE
A TRUE NONDUALITY YOU HAVE TO ACCEPT
WHAT APPEARS AS DUALITY. Nothing is
either/or. Double think.*

The next clue was late in coming to me. If I had discovered it earlier I could have saved myself a lot of confusion
and frustration, because it is a very practical working clue.
Many times I tried to apply truths that I knew were correct
and valid ones, but the results didn't come out the way they
were supposed to. Finally I found the key. Everything at the
finite level, the level of human thought, needs something to
complete it, to make it whole. Man needs woman, plus
needs minus, knowledge has to be coupled with experience
to make it practical. The same thing applies to truth.

There is no truth, though absolutely true in itself, that
stands by itself when it is applied at the finite level. Every
truth needs a complementary (complete-a-mentary) truth to
make it applicable. For instance, in the spiritual life surrender
is an absolute necessity, but surrender alone is not enough.
What is one surrendering to? Fear, ignorance, dark forces?

No. Surrender must be complemented by a concept of God or life worthy of being surrendered to. But on the other hand, many good people study beautiful concepts of God on Sunday which they don't know how to surrender to during the rest of the week; so their concepts remain in their heads and mean nothing.

Once again, this fits the two commandments. Jesus gave us two complementary truths; they must go together. The love of God is nothing without being expressed as the love of neighbor and vice versa. Or as St. James said, "Faith, if it hath not works, is dead, being alone." Faith is an absolute, but it doesn't stand alone; it needs action.

At the finite level there are no absolute truths which work by themselves; so we should always ask ourselves: What truth complements this one? Then, combining the two, we will have, perhaps for the first time, the formula for successful living.

> *Contemplate the clue: Everything at the finite level needs a complementary truth to make it work.*

Next, we must penetrate further into the meaning of relativity itself. As individuals we each have within us elements of the primitive man who lived by superstition and ritual as well as elements of the Aristotelian absolute way of thinking which evolved later. We have now arrived individually at the place the world has collectively, at the need to make these two sides relate.

In fact, the world will destroy itself now if it doesn't learn how to make the two sides relate, and so will we. It has always been said in the past that a person couldn't be both a mystic and a householder, that he had to be one or the other. But now the householder or material side has invented a technology which can destroy the world unless mankind becomes both a mystic and a businessman at the same time.

I smile when I say that, because just as we have now grown into the ability to double think, it is no accident that our technology has advanced to this stage at this time. Both the world and the individual are now ready and able to live by relativity.

It's necessary to comprehend at least a slight understanding of the material aspect of relativity before comprehending the spiritual implications. For centuries the world took Euclid's word for it that two straight lines never cross, but up popped Einstein, whose theories imply that such lines do cross and that time and space are relative. He showed us that there are no positions in the universe which are absolutely stationary, therefore no set position from which absolute time or shape and measurement of an object can be ascertained.

In other words, the earth revolves around the sun. But the sun is also moving, so there is never any time when we are in the same spot. The earth moves at an approximate rate of 67,000 miles an hour; so, although we think we are standing still, what was "here" or "there" a few seconds ago is now thousands of miles from where it was then. "Here" becomes a relative term. It is "here" in relation to something else, but not here in an absolute sense.

According to Einstein's theories, physical objects become transformed into fields of electrical force, of energy, depending on the velocity of their travel. Theoretically by the time an object reaches the speed of light it is transformed into light. This makes a body or object relative to the speed it is moving and destroys the static nature of material things.

Naturally all of this is just so many words to us as humans. We still live and react in the human time and space continuum. But it is good for us to touch on it because it shakes our belief that we are really comprehending the truth of things with our finite senses. We can start to realize that objects are never independent of the conditions affecting the observer. And no two times, places, or anything else are exactly alike. All intellectual knowledge suffers from being relative and becomes no more than a cat chasing its tail unless one senses the relativity of things.

In its most esoteric or spiritual sense, relativity tells us a number of things. It says: Motion is relative, not absolute, which means that as a man I am a finite being expressing the infinite through motion which is relative to me, not absolute. Therefore my humanity is relative, not absolute. It says: The velocity of light is constant, which is like saying that all men have a constant source to call upon or relate to, that all men are equal in the sight of God. And it says: The mass of a body in motion varies with the velocity, which implies that I, as a human, am mass, and that I vary, change in form and even in appearance, as my motion or vibration increases or decreases. As I reach higher spiritual levels my body changes.

There is no time but the moment of NOW, and that is relative to the individual. So in all areas of life, if I am able to see the relative nature of persons, places, things, and situations, I am seeing reality or total truth.

> *I live in truth when I am able to sense the relative*
> *nature of my own being, how close to the source,*
> *how slow in matter. I flow with the ever-changing*
> *sea of relativity.*

At this point we come up against something called "law" —Law as opposed to Grace. (When I talk about law I am referring to man-made laws, not divine or spiritual law.) The dictionary says that laws are rules, principles to which all must conform. Law assumes there is a standard by which things can be measured, that there are times, places, situations, even people, which are alike. But what about relativity? We just found out that no two situations or people are alike. Obviously relativity and law are in conflict.

Law came into being because people didn't know how to live spiritually, didn't understand relativity. It was an expediency, the best man could come up with. No one argues with the goals law sets out to achieve—harmony, individual rights, well-being for all—but now if our society is to gain a more truthful and honest way of living we have to go beyond the law. Until we evolve beyond our humanity we have to live by relativity.

I think society has been trying to do that in a way. In recent years we have tried to take care of the exceptions to the law, but we've passed so many laws doing it that we've almost rendered all law useless. Any skillful lawyer can get anyone off of almost anything.

Jesus understood the conflict between law and relativity. That's why he proposed another way of living. He called his way GRACE. He said that the only way to truly fulfill the aims of law was to live by grace. Grace is infinitely individual. Grace applies honestly to each person at each moment in whatever terms the relative need assumes. Since the only truly righteous judgment is relative, you might say that grace and relativity are the *same word*.

When I understood this I felt a lot better about myself. For years I felt an instinctive reaction to laws, that somehow they were not honest, that law couldn't be spiritual. I often found times when I felt it was right to break the law, and that bothered me. Now I know that I was trying to envision a higher way of life, one lived by grace.

We'd all like to live by grace, but there is a paradox. Grace, or relativity, is impossible to live by intellectually because there are no laws pertaining to it. It is possible for us to learn man-made laws with our minds and live by them. That's why society formulated them. But when we bump into relativity, there isn't anything the mind can use. You might say about relativity that *the center is everywhere;* however there is nothing in that statement which gives direction to the mind.

Another way of putting it is this. Law is linear, but life itself is a cluster. Cluster is multidimensional, involving all levels in all directions. Grace or infinity is not flat or one-dimensional. It is cluster. As the center is everywhere, life radiates out from each one of *us* as centers. In order to live as cluster we have to arrive, through right identification, at action based on relativity, which can relate only to now. Only in the now or at the time of action can we sense the relative situation and respond in a truly honest way. We can't prejudge. Law is past and future based on a linear position, but *now* is grace or cluster.

Don't be discouraged, though. Jesus not only told us to live by cluster by giving us the two commandments; he also gave us a hint on how to do it. He told us to have a priority list. Although he gave us two commandments, he said, "Love God. This is the first and great commandment." In other words, in order to sense a relative situation, we should start by first checking in with the absolute, the source, or the spiritual truth of the situation. When we have related to that aspect we can make better sense out of the finite side and see its relation to the absolute.

The other day my stereo broke down; nothing came out of the speakers. I began by wasting a lot of time checking the speakers and their lines. Then I looked at the turntable, on and on, until I finally looked at the amplifier, the source of all. The breakdown was there. I should have known that since everything related first and foremost to the amplifier, checking that should have been at the top of my priority list.

Einstein formulated his theories by assuming his goal was possible and working back from that rather than starting with the obstacles as most scientists did. Jung advised checking in with the collective unconscious and then relating it through dreams and such to the personal. Teilhard and Goldsmith taught us to experience God and then relate it to the earth.

The Oriental study of Yin and Yang does the same. I really understood the true Yin and Yang macrobiotic diet when I realized this.The diet shows that all food falls under either the Yin side, which represents acidity, sugar, fruits, and so on—the foods that expand—or the Yang, which is alkaloid, salt, cereals—which contract. Most often, it is necessary to have more Yin than Yang for a *balanced* diet, but the combination is always changing and relative. The balance changes with the seasons, with the climate, with local crops, and with the individual. No food is totally bad, but each is healthful when it is balanced with the proper amount of the opposite. There is no set law; it is relative. But the Yin and Yang also have a priority list; one should start with the pure or positive side as a base and edge up to a balance by adding the negative or Yang. This is the same as starting with God and adding neighbor. This is a *grace* diet.

The whole grace or relativity trip is not, thank goodness, a mental one. You don't have to live by a whole head full of thoughts or laws. You just have to know the *next* one, and that isn't too hard for any of us. We always know what we have to do *next*. At least there is a way we can know what is next on the priority list, and that is by meditating. In fact, it is impossible to live by spirit without meditating. We let the facts fill our head, but then we meditate and tune into the relative next step.

*Relativity and Grace are the same. Grace is cluster, and cluster transcends law. Relativity is lived by priority—first relating to the source or God, and then to action or the personal.*

A few years ago as I became more in tune with relativity and life all around began to speed up more and more, I began to realize I was facing a new problem. Before that time I had always been able to decide on how much energy and time I would need to get something done. If I felt I had enough of both time and energy I could turn on the faucet and let it flow. When I was finished I could turn off the faucet and let my supply of energy build up again. But a few years ago I began to realize that as everything around me was speeding up I could no longer think in terms of accomplishing specific objectives in the way I had.

For instance, if I wanted to write a book in the past, I would get the decks cleared, take off a couple of months, and do it. But now, in contact with so many levels of being, with so many people, unexpected calls, and even unexpected turns of events, long before I could get a book finished it might have turned into a whole new ball game. Simple things could become endless, and the bucket to be filled with energy could become a bottomless one.

I found that this day of change or relativity demanded a whole new way of living. Instead of focusing outwardly on a definite external objective, I now had to focus on the flow of energy from within. Again, attention to the source became top priority. My concern became maintaining the flow, not external results. Whereas in the past my eye was on the finishing of a book, now it had to be on the *now*, on keeping the flow of energy coming no matter what the end would be. I had to know myself well enough to be aware of just how far I could open the faucet of my energies. If I could maintain my realization of oneness with infinite energy, the results would take care of themselves, but if I started to fight change or look at results, I found myself cut off and depleted.

In the past change was something to which we adjusted. When a change came we would hear people say, "All right, I will take care of that. I will adjust to the change. I will fit it into the old pattern." They could say that because we had a society which was created by laws outlining what was thought to be a permanent state. Changes were simply forced into the pattern and frozen there.

But today our society is obviously in a state of chaos and confusion brought on by the day of relativity: laws and patterns no longer work, and no laws fit all people and situations. If we expect to live by relativity, we have to realize that *change must become a way of life,* something we flow or grow with rather than something we resist.

If you are one of those who find an inner compulsion to keep moving it isn't because you want to run away; it's just that at some level you realize that the old security-based pattern of living no longer fits in a world of constant change. The desire to keep moving is the desire to learn how to live with change as a way of life because that's the way the world of the future will be.

This confusion of change is often called future shock, but few realize the spiritual implications of future shock. The new day is the day of relativity as opposed to law; so *future shock is the shock of moving from law to grace*. It is the shock of speeding up from separateness into oneness.

We are like spokes of a wheel. Each of us is individual, each has a separate identity, each a different color, but as the wheel speeds up, bit by bit all spokes begin to appear as though they were one. Varying colors become fused into one color, then whirl into light, one light for all—just as all matter becomes light when it is increased in speed.

> *Take a moment to digest this. Contemplate what it means for CHANGE TO BE A WAY OF LIFE rather than something we adjust to. (Don't forget to make notes in your journal of anything that comes out of your own meditation. They will be far more important to you than what I have voiced because they will be your own consciousness.)*

If the kingdom of heaven exists at all it has to be right here and right now. If we are not aware of it, that doesn't mean it's nonexistent; it means we don't know what it is. It's relative. We don't recognize it mainly because we've been sold a bill of goods, the same bill of goods that makes living by relativity impossible. In order to expose this clue and lay open the lie we've been handed, we have to attack one of society's most sacred cows: a belief that perfection is desirable. Or, I should say, the belief that there is any such thing as absolute perfection at the human level.

I could manufacture a million objects, say a million water glasses. On the shelf they would all look exactly alike, but under a microscope you'd see that each one is a tiny bit different. Which is the perfect one? If you said one was perfect, that would mean that you were putting down, condemning, the other 999,999 as though they were inferior to the perfect one.

Because this perfection stunt was pulled in terms of Jesus, the greatest load of guilt or hate possible was fed to mankind. When we were told that Jesus was perfect and that we should be like him or feel guilty, we were doomed. He was perfect, all right, but not in the way we were led to believe. He was perfect because he was perfectly what a growing, evolving, living man should be. But he wasn't flawless in finite terms. He stumbled, he fell, he cried. Just as you and I do. He wasn't on top of things all the time. In the end he made it all the way to perfection, but he had to work at it just as you and I do. "Why callest thou *me* good [perfect]?" Jesus asked. "There is none good but one, and that is God [the infinite invisible nature of self]."

Perfection at the absolute level means one thing, but it means something entirely different at the finite or relative level. Again, at the finite level everything needs something to complete it, so if you judge perfection as being completely whole and flawless, then everything at the finite level is sinful or incomplete. The truth is that at the finite level it is perfect to be imperfect. Perfection does exist at the absolute level, so *we should be idealists aiming at perfection, but not perfectionists expecting it in finite terms.*

We have to realize what a mistake it is to expect perfection at the third dimension. Perfection is the hatchet man of law. Laws dominate individuality and set up standards by which to measure man. All who don't conform to that standard are chopped down by the myth of perfection. *The belief that perfection is desirable makes living by relativity impossible.*

Many of us think we are spiritual because we have found out that perfection is the truth of all being (which is true in absolute terms), but we then expect to see it in finite terms and judge its absence as bad. Unconsciously, we judge everyone (including ourselves) because we inevitably see imperfections in everyone at the human level.

Jesus not only refused to condemn others for having flaws, but he also hinted that we needed them. He said that through our sins we are made WHOLE. If we were already flawless we wouldn't appear at this level—so sin is needed to complete us.

That word "sin" opens up a big can of beans. To be free we should know what sin really is and what its purpose is.

I like to refer to sins or imperfections as stumbling blocks. Anything that is difficult, inharmonious, painful, bothersome, frustrating, or destructive is a kind of sin. That's more or less what Jung was getting at when he came up with the word "shadows" in attempting to find a term that wouldn't imply morality but could be used to identify the stumbling blocks. Jung said the shadow side represented "the repressed tendencies of all those characteristics the existence of which are found to be painful or regrettable." He said that shadows must be accepted and understood as an adjunct of our egos, for only then can we give them their true place in wholeness, relativity.

When, in our fear of imperfection, we refuse to recognize shadows in ourselves, we project them onto others, and that creates paranoia. We even apply shadows to groups, and before long we are attacking whole races and colors. But when we know the necessity of shadows, realize that they do have a purpose, we can assimilate them. Sins in themselves are not good, but they serve a vital function, and until we understand their purpose we live in a godless world of duality.

Shadows exist only on our way to the light. Once we are in the light we *are* the light, and there are no more shadows, no more imperfections. Shadows indicate which way the light is; they are in the opposite direction from the light. If we didn't have shadows we wouldn't know which way to go to reach the light.

But there is a more practical way of explaining it. Realize that there is no act of creativity which doesn't require what appears to be an act of destruction. If I want to build a house I have to cut the trees down. If you see me cutting trees down, you might think I am imperfect, that I am a "sinner," but if you see the new house you'd say I was perfect and a "saint" for building such a nice place.

The day-to-day problem of coping with creative tension is what makes life worth living to begin with. When there is no creative tension to put stimulation into life, boredom sets in. I recently had dinner with a man in Tokyo who is considered the number two master of flower arrangement in Japan. We discussed the trinitylike three basic elements in Zen-inspired floral arrangement. These are called the *Shin, Soe,* and *Hiki.* He pointed out that these three basic elements of life make the arrangement interesting because they are *out of balance.* "Symmetry," he said, "is dull." Imbalance, movement, and imperfection make man and art interesting and *alive.* There is nothing creative in balance; perfect balance is motionless and dead. It's boring.

Now hold on—*double think.* No one is trying to say that sins or shadows are fun, no one is trying to excuse imperfection, no one is trying to open the door for everyone to go out and commit all the selfish acts possible. We should aim at perfection, but on the way realize that flaws are the complement to growth. For that matter, I'll throw a seeming contradiction at you: *Shadows are not real.* I've just been saying they are valuable, and they are, but now I remind you that they are fiction. They are only the absence of light. They exist only at the relative level—but we never transcend this level without admitting them and using them.

Jung also said that we need this human level because only at this level is consciousness expanded, only at the flesh level is there fuel for growth. Our object is to grow, to expand our consciousness until we rise to the stature of Christs.

Most people think that if they don't sin, don't break any laws, they are fulfilling their responsibility as human beings. But they are not fulfilling their responsibility as spiritual beings—to grow into the new man, fully human, beyond both bad and good, to live by relativity, not law.

Instead of mistakenly believing perfection is desirable, instead of rejecting the life-giving necessity of imperfection, instead of rejecting our physical bodies because they appear imperfect, instead of wanting perfection in others, let us stop fearing shadows and start welcoming life.

As Teilhard wrote in *Hymn of the Universe:*

*Blessed be you, mighty matter, irresistible march of evolution, reality ever new-born; you who, by constantly shattering our mental categories, force us to go ever further and further in our pursuit of the truth.*

*Without you, without your onslaughts, without your uprootings of us, we should remain all our lives inert, stagnant, puerile, ignorant both of ourselves and of God. You who batter us and then dress our wounds, you who resist us and yield to us, you who wreck and build, you who shackle and liberate, the sap of our souls, the hand of God, the flesh of Christ: it is you, matter, that I bless.*

*I bless you, matter, and you I acclaim: not as the pontiffs of science or the moralizing preachers depict you, debased, disfigured—a mass of brute forces and base appetites—but as you reveal yourself to me today, in your totality and your true nature.*

# THE
# LOVE STORY

All the clues we have touched on so far have one thing in common: they are all designed to free us from the mind. Whether we like it or not, we are prisoners of the mind. We want to love, but our mind has kept us from it. The mind itself isn't bad. It's just an instrument, neither bad nor good. But, like a computer, when it is programmed with ignorance it produces results based on that ignorance.

Anything that can imprison us can also free us; so our aim is to understand the mind's true purpose and use, not eliminate, it. Edgar Cayce said, "The spirit is the life. Mind is the builder. The physical is the result." Many have quoted him out of context, saying, "Mind is the builder," without adding that the spirit is the life force. Mind alone is not the builder; it is a tool we build with. It is the complement of spirit.

We all create our lives according to the way our minds are conditioned. From the time we are born, the beliefs inherent in society, what we are fed in schools, the propaganda Madison Avenue concocts, and all kinds of things have pumped programming into our mental computers, and we act accordingly.

I know you don't like to think you are not a free agent. It hurts to think you are brainwashed, but if you were not out of touch with your true self you wouldn't be facing an identity dilemma, you wouldn't have to search for the treasure—you'd "see" it.

We study the life of Jesus because we sense that he was completely unbrainwashed, and we want to be that way ourselves. Because his mind was unconditioned he could say, "I and my Father are one," without qualifying it as you and I would do. Paul said we too could be free if we would "have that mind which was in Christ Jesus." So let's see what kind of a mind that was.

Jesus didn't use his mind as a "thinking" instrument. Rational thinking is the mother of law. Intellectually reaching back into the past for facts which are relative to the past and projecting them into the future precludes the relativity of *now*. That's why Jesus said, "Take no thought for the morrow" or the past.

Jesus used his mind as a "seeing" instrument, not as an instrument to rationalize with. He used his mind as an avenue of awareness, as a channel through which his sense of the infinite interpreted the finite. By "seeing" the truth of people he freed them.

Thinking doesn't free anyone, but "seeing" does, and that is the basis of spiritual healing. When truth is seen, the hypnotism of false identity is broken and the person is freed. The mind, properly used, sees the relative nature of now and relates God to the present.

When the mind is cluttered with old concepts it is opaque, but when it is a *transparency,* the pure light of truth can be seen through it. Pure creation is produced. Jesus' mind was such a pure transparency for God that it was used only for "loving," "seeing," or "knowing."

There it is—the key. The key to the word "love," and therefore the whole message of the New Testament, is the word KNOW. Literally, to love is to know. Love is not an emotion. It is the capacity to KNOW or see the true nature of a person or of God. When Jesus gave us the commandments to love God and neighbor, he was saying: Know them, resolve the identity dilemma, translate appearances into reality.

Whenever you read the New Testament with that in mind, always translating the word "love" into "know," the veil is removed and the whole map is clear.

See how this applies in your present personal life. Pick out the person you feel loves you the most, and you will find that it is the person you feel *knows* you the best. It is a person who sees you in a double thread manner, one who is aware of your humanity and its limitations but who constantly relates it to your divine potential as well. You don't feel you are really loved by someone who totally ignores your

humanity—you are always afraid of what he will think when
he sees your clay feet. Also, you don't feel loved by anyone
who sees *only* your humanity because you know you are
also divine and perfect as well. The person who loves you
the best is the person who knows you fully, understands the
relative nature of things, and therefore doesn't judge you.
You feel that those who love you know you, but you also
feel that if anyone would take the time to really know you,
he, too, would love you.

> *Our goal is to use the mind as a "seeing" instru-
> ment, for seeing is loving, and to love is to KNOW.*

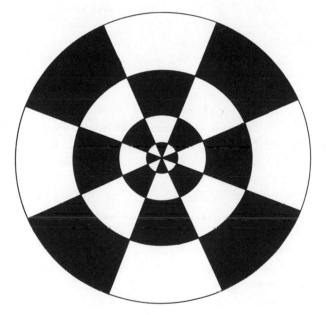

Having deciphered the clues for loving, we continue our
"love affair" where Jesus told us to. We start with the first
commandment on the priority list: to know God. Frankly, it's
harder to know God than it is our neighbor because God
can't be located in time or space. It's infinite and everywhere, and a finite mind cannot contain infinity. That's why
the Orientals say about God, "If you can name it, it isn't.'
The one disagreement I had with a Tibetan lama friend of

mine was over the word "God." He urged me to avoid the word altogether because it had been so vastly distorted and misused that it was worthless and stood in the way of true awareness. Well, I agree that the word is almost completely misunderstood in the Western world and that most Westerners are conditioned to think of God in theistic terms: as though God were an all-powerful ruler separate and apart from ourselves. But I don't agree that because most people use the word incorrectly, we should avoid it. To avoid using the word "God" would be to reject the key clue to our map. Instead, we must eliminate our misconception (our brainwashing) and experience a true concept of God. It doesn't matter if others misinterpret the word. We must use all our strength to "see" God because "to know God aright is life eternal" and that is what we are here to achieve.

Although we may not wish to take our Oriental friends' advice to avoid the word "God," we can greatly profit by listening to the words they use in place of the word. Two of the most important are the words "Braham" and "Om." Whenever Orientals explain those words they are always deliberately careful to boggle the mind so it can't finitize God or make a person out of it. They make the words so all-inclusive that they encompass everything, the beginning and the end, nothing and all. Therefore, it is impossible to see God as a single supreme being. It is supreme "beingness," but can't be localized as a superman.

I think the best synonym for God is the Chinese word *Tao,* which translates as "the way." When we think of God as the true way of life, the infinite way, we have freed ourselves from theism. The idea of God as the way implies that God is the creative principle of life (the actual principle) and is therefore never apart from its creation. Also, God can never create anything unlike itself and therefore is never duality.

Theism creates absolutes and rejects the world. On the other hand, its opposite, pantheism, correctly believes that the world is the manifestation of God but ends up rejecting the whole for the parts, begins to worship forms rather than the thing that created them. Actually, theism and pantheism complement each other. Put the two together, and you have a concept of God that relates totally at all levels.

I believe that our Christian map gives us three words for God which make God infinite and yet relate it to the world.

The three words, OMNIPOTENT, OMNIPRESENT, and OMNISCIENT, are the next three clues.

OMNIPOTENT means the *only* power. All power. It means that all energy, all cause, all motivating force is God. Because God is omnipotent, there is no cause or power in the universe except God.

God is the power that holds itself in uninterrupted completeness as the whole universe. God is the power that maintains, sustains, supports, and governs itself as the completeness that is the universe. God is the power that is continuously self-sustaining, self-maintaining, as every planet and being.

God is an impersonal loving principle functioning as the activity of the universe *constantly* in perfect order. There is never a mistake. There is nothing haphazard about the divine order of omnipotence.

In explaining the omnipotence of God, Joel Goldsmith pointed out that there is a kind of contradiction in using the word "power." Power implies power over something. If God is all, what is there to be a power over? In that respect God is a *nonpower.* It is the only power, in that all movement of creativity is God. God being *all* there is, there is nothing to oppose it.

Do you see what this does to us when we try to call on God to overcome some evil power? We're just being stupid. If God is all power, what is there for it to be over? To ask God to overcome itself would be like expecting one hand to slap our other hand; both hands belong to the same power. The minute we think of God as a great power which heals or performs miracles, we are not loving God because we are not believing that God is omnipotent. The minute we call on God to "do" anything, we are being theistic, even though we believe we do not conceive of a theistic God.

Whenever a person says, "God help me," he shows he thinks there is a power apart from God's, that God permits him to live. We live because God's power expresses itself *as* us. We can't help living; nor can God help being the power in our life. There are not two lives, not two powers. There is one life, and this life is God living its own life as us.

I may be jumping the gun a bit, but I would like to tell the story of an experience I had which helped me get over believing in God as a power over evil. Before this time I didn't know God because, though I believed intellectually that God is the only power, I didn't "see" it.

One day I was in a bad down. All morning I called on everything I knew to pull me out of it. I prayed, but nothing worked. After many hours I just gave up and sat staring in front of myself. Finally my eyes focused on a light bulb. I saw that the light came from the action and interaction of the negative and positive forces which produce electricity. You might say that to my human sense the light was caused by the action of two powers, plus and minus. Both were necessary in order to create light. I had been praying that the bad would go away. Then I realized that if I were successful in my prayers, there wouldn't be any light because both positive and negative forces were needed.

Suddenly it dawned on me that there weren't two powers. There was really only one, the power of electricity. It, in turn, expressed itself out here in the finite world as two powers, but in fact there was only one cause. What I saw with my human eyes was not duality or two powers, but really polarity—complementary aspects of the one. Electricity wasn't being a power over anything, it was just expressing itself, and I was blessed with light. In fact, it wasn't even being a power over darkness. Darkness has no power. Darkness (whether in the mind of man or in the world) is the absence of power, the absence of God. It doesn't make any difference if one takes a birthday candle or a searchlight into a dark closet; darkness has no power to put out the light. Light—or God—is the only power, and although it appears to us at the finite level in pairs (just as our two commandments come in a pair), in the invisible there is only one.

So, in absolute terms, there is no evil power, there is no power at all really, just God "being." When the ancient Hebrews said, "The Lord God is ONE," they knew what they were talking about; it's a pity they didn't take it far enough. Indeed, whenever we believe in other powers, we are worshiping graven images, setting up separate powers.

We love God by refusing to believe that there are powers apart from God. When we know God as the only power, we love God.

When we know that the men in the Pentagons of the world have no power apart from God, we are loving God. When we know that germs can't destroy life because God's

is the only power, we are loving God. When we know that
power isn't in good or bad foods, we are loving God.

In other words, we can check our every thought, and
whenever we see we have been tricked into believing that
there is any power other than God's we can realize we've
been brainwashed by that belief. We can refuse to fight the
appearance, get rid of the ignorance, and be in love with
God.

Now we know that when Jesus said we should "resist not
evil" he was telling us how to love God. He was saying that
whenever we remember that God is the only power we are
loving God.

*God is OMNIPOTENT.*

The next word, OMNIPRESENCE. Omnipresence is really
just another way of saying omnipotence. It means that God
is everywhere—everywhereness. It means you can't run
from God, you can't hide from God, you can't escape God,

nor is God ever apart from you; God is ever available, is ever there to behold you.

If we say that God is everywhere, what does it mean? Some of you might say, "That's simple, God is the whole universe." That is true, there is no greater truth, but it isn't enough to make that statement if you leave yourself out. Believe me, you are never going to know your own identity if you don't realize God's everythingness includes *you.* When you see that God is the whole universe, you can include yourself; but you can't know yourself until you see that by being omnipresent, God is present *as* you. There is no such thing as unexpressed God. There is no such thing as unidentified God. All substance, form, or activity is God being omnipresent.

There wouldn't be any evidence that God existed if there were no forms or substance. What evidence would there be that God *is* life? So, as God is all life, it is all form everywhere. There is no use saying "God is all" unless you perceive that God is the entirety of the universe, all of it. God is the identity of everything and everyone in existence. It is as simple as that.

But that too isn't quite enough. In order to look at the forms and see them free of brainwashing we must realize that God is always being *itself,* not something other than itself. No matter what the specific nature of the identity appears as, no matter how it is named or misnamed, it is still God being itself *as* that appearance. What's more, no special species are more God-appearing than others. Animals, fish, fowl, trees, flowers, plants, and everything else are God appearing infinitely, omnipresent, as all. God is all existence. God is all variety.

The clue here for our practical realization is this: it's possible for us to understand each other's identity, but first we must feel, see, and experience the infinite omnipresent nature of each other; *then* we can know or love the appearance. It is absolutely essential to perceive what God is in relation to all existence before we can perceive what God is as the existence of the specific identity. That includes our concept of our own self as well.

What a mockery it is to pray to bring the light of God (everywhereness) into our presence! It was never apart from us, and if anything, our prayers push us further out of love with God, further out of "knowing" God is everywhere. In fact, when we feel the presence of God, see God in the sunset, on the wave, or expressed in a flower, we are recognizing God's omnipresence and are loving. It's a pity we don't look at a prison, at a crippled body, or at a slum and know the same thing. You know what would happen if we did? They'd start to change because they would have been freed by the love of God. To believe that God is omnipresent in this particular spot is to bring love into the situation, and love brings freedom. (Check and see if you've read this last page or so without thinking of God as a supreme being. Are you still thinking of God as a superperson? If so, it's up to you to remind yourself of the true meaning every time you see the word.)

*God is OMNIPRESENCE.*

The third of the three words attributed to God: OMNIS-CIENT. Omniscient means that God is all-knowing, all intelligence infinitely expressed. Let's go back to the universe again for a moment. There is some order in the universe, some intelligence operating the whole works, just as there is some intelligence operating our individual bodies. This universal intelligence or mind doesn't argue or quarrel; it knows no fear. It is calm, peaceful, and orderly. Every truth of the universe is universal truth; every truth of the universe is true of your universe right where you are. When you know a truth, it isn't that you are knowing the truth about the stars and planets—you are knowing the truth about *truth*. You are tuned in to the one omnipresent all-truth. It is a simple matter to realize that the same intelligence that is operating the universe is operating yours as well, right now, right here, at this moment.

This omniscient, all-knowing intelligence is responsible only for itself. You are not responsible for it. Intelligence is responsible for being intelligent as your own intelligence if you let it. You can depend on this ever-present intelligence to act intelligently as you. You can depend on it to act as everyone in the world when you identify it and them. Your only concern is just to keep right on realizing that intelligence is omniscient, omnipresent, omnipotent, and it will appear as everything and everyone in your universe.

Let that mind that is God reveal itself to be your only mind, and then you are being that mind which was in Christ Jesus.

Do you see what a mockery this makes out of our trying to tell God what's up? If God is all-knowing, what makes us believe that we have to inform all-knowingness, all-intelligence, of anything? How ridiculous we are when we believe we have to say the right words in order to make God understand and come to our aid, or to inform God of our needs. Prayers which inform God of our problems imply that God is some kind of half-wit who is unable to keep up with his creation and needs our help to keep him on the ball.

The truth of the matter is that of the three words I have outlined for God, *omniscient* is the most loving word of all. As I said, to love is to know; so God, seen as all-intelligence, is therefore all-loving. God is pure knowing, pure love. When we hear the statement "God is love," that is exactly what it means.

It is fine to light a candle, it is fine to say a prayer or a particular mantra as a communion with God, but a person doing any of those things in order to inform God or reach out to God, as though God weren't all-knowing and ever present, is actually denying God.

*God is OMNISCIENCE.*

Having contemplated God in absolute terms, for God is absolute, we come to one of the two most confusing and difficult clues in the entire map, how to find an absolute God in the human scene. The trick is that we shouldn't try—that's where more people have foundered than any other place. *God is not in the human scene.*

Another way of saying that is: Absolutes don't exist at the finite level. As long as we try to look for absolutes, for God, in finite terms we not only end up failures but we end up losing faith in God entirely. It can be no other way. We can relate the absolute to the finite world, but we can't find it there.

Jesus tried to explain that God was not in the human scene when he said, "My kingdom is not of this world." But because he didn't elaborate on it fully or because he didn't get it across, the whole Christian message almost went on the rocks. People thought he meant that his kingdom was a miserable place of sackcloth and ashes, where good things were denied, or else that his kingdom was off in space apart from the earth, perhaps with streets of gold and fluffy angel wings. But that isn't what he meant, and we must discover his true meaning or we will never be able to love God.

"My kingdom is not of this world" is a double sentence with two complementary phrases: "my kingdom" and "this world." We know what his kingdom was—it was the kingdom of God, where absolutes, perfection, and harmony exist—but we can't understand the clue unless we know what he meant by "this world."

"This world" is false material sense, ignorance, and misconception. It believes people and things are no more than what they appear to the senses. When Jesus said his kingdom was not of this world, he didn't say it wasn't of the earth. He wasn't putting down the planet. He was trying to say his kingdom was not a mistaken or brainwashed *concept* of this planet. He was saying that his kingdom was not of a false sense of materiality, of wrong identification.

When Jesus said, "I have overcome the world," he didn't say, "I have overcome the earth." He loved the earth: "The earth is the Lord's and the fullness thereof." He knew that the earth was the kingdom of God, just as the body is the temple of the living God. But he knew we wouldn't truly know or love the earth as long as we were brainwashed into a false sense of our bodies and the earth.

He not only told us where his kingdom wasn't—in the material concept of things—but he told us where it was—within. He certainly didn't mean that we had a whole world inside our bodies. He meant that the capacity to "see" the earth with right identification is *potential* within each of us. As long as we thrash around with our minds trying to look at a material world in order to discover heaven, we are just whistling "Dixie." When we know that each one of us at any moment can turn within our own consciousness and see or experience the truth, we find the real kingdom.

The whole of God is bound up in the word CONSCIOUSNESS. All three of our descriptive words—omnipresence, omnipotence, omniscience—are included in one word, consciousness. I am not talking about our finite awareness, not the limitations of our knowledge in our confused state, but about our very life itself.

There is a process which replenishes the cells in our body and functions as all the activities of our body. That same consciousness directs our growth, goes before us to make the crooked places straight, is the intelligence of our bodies and talents which surrounds us constantly, has provided for us all our lives. Whatever that is, it is consciousness. Our consciousness. And because there is only one consciousness, our consciousness is God's consciousness.

For instance, a mother doesn't know how to make a fingernail on her child's hand, yet the child's own consciousness knows how because his consciousness is all-knowing, all-powerful, and ever present. The consciousness that holds the stars in the heavens, the consciousness that regulates the seasons, that contains all intelligence, is actually your own consciousness, the same consciousness that is within me.

*When I know that I have a maintaining, fulfilling, sustaining consciousness within me I know where "my kingdom" is.*

Consciousness is always expressed outwardly and should be; although we seek to find the kingdom within, we can relate it to the without, to the earth. I've heard people express that in a great way. They use the word "earth" as though it is a verb. When they want to find the material application for a spiritual truth they say, "Earth that for us." Instead of wasting time saying some complicated sentence such as: "Consciousness expresses itself in form, therefore the materialization of that consciousness in pure terms is . . . ," it's much simpler to say, "It's earthed as . . ." But remember, when you say "earth it" you mean the pure material expression of God seen at the earth level, not the "this world" concept of matter.

The "this world" which Jesus said we should overcome is very much like the false sense of the earth which the Orientals call maya or illusion. Maya presupposes that we are hypnotized by our senses into a false belief in what we see. Most of you are familiar with teachings which prove that our senses are so limited and distorted that although they tell us a bit about things, so much is left out or twisted that the appearance is a lie. But there is a difference between thinking that everything is illusion and realizing that the illusion is in our heads, not in reality.

Many believe that the whole picture is illusion and that when one experiences samadi or nirvana, the whole thing vanishes. But unless a person realizes that the only thing which disappears is the *illusion,* and that something remains in its place, he is in danger of rejecting the world of form. And you know what happens. Anything you reject rejects you in return; so many of those who incorrectly understand the theory of maya end up producing a world of misery and poverty.

Correctly understood, Jesus implied that man had to overcome wrong identification about himself and the world, that this wrong identification was a lie, but that when the illusion was eliminated and one saw through a glass brightly, or truly, one beheld a world of form right here where the illusion had been.

Be sure you are clear on this. There is form, there are people and things, but they are not what we think they are when we are confused by a "this world" concept of matter, when we forget relativity and that forms change with motion or vibration.

We do have forms. The Christ did have a form called Jesus. The mistake is in getting the two sides confused or in trying to eliminate either side. The body is an effect—an effect that has been created by consciousness. Everything we see, hear, touch, taste, smell, or identify in the visible world of forms is an effect. The materialistic viewpoint is the one which takes things at face value, forgetting where the true identity lies.

There is cause (God) and the effect. So, finally, in order to put the seal on our understanding of God, in order to really love God, we come to the second most difficult clue. This is a clue on top of a clue because it is impossible to really see "this world," the world of effect, for what it is without understanding this point. *There is no cause in effect* —otherwise God would not be omnipotent.

No clue is more grossly misunderstood than this. In fact, the entire world sense is based on this misunderstanding. Let me explain. I am saying that nothing you can see or touch has *any* power, none at all. I mean this literally. There is not a single cause in anything you can see.

For instance, no bullet ever killed anyone. A bullet has not intelligence. It is just an effect, and no effect has any power. If I put a bullet on the table, it will stay there a hundred years or more unless someone moves it. The bullet has no power to move. If some idiot takes the bullet and puts it in a gun and fires it, the bullet may be hurled through space and enter someone's body, but the bullet didn't kill the person. The consciousness of the one who made the bullet, put it in the gun, and fired it did the killing. It is a "this world" belief to think the bullet has power.

We even believe that people can die from heart failure, or from a faulty liver or lung. This isn't true. Hearts, livers, and lungs are effects. They have no intelligence and no power to cause anything. As long as the creative force of consciousness is there, a heart will function, but when the consciousness is removed, the heart stops.

Medical science has been made painfully aware of this lately. Although a few heart transplants have been successful, the great majority fail because replacing one effect with another doesn't do the trick. Unless the consciousness of life is restimulated in the patient, it is only a matter of time before he dies. A new heart can be like a new battery: it will run for a while, but if the short hasn't been repaired the battery will not be restored and will soon wear out. It is "this world" to believe that a heart has the power to kill.

Heroin and alcohol are also just effects. Heroin is not bad and it's not good; it is just an effect, it just is. Actually, heroin is the result of heroin consciousness. If a person's consciousness utilizes heroin in the wrong way, his consciousness will kill him, but it is not the heroin which did it. It is "this world" to believe heroin has power.

It's surprising how many people just can't rise above believing effects are either bad or good. Not too long ago I had to address a group of well-intended citizens who met before breakfast each morning to discuss drug abuse problems in their city. In my talk I said that the young didn't want to put anything down, that they knew nothing was bad or good in itself but that anything could be used for bad. I thought my statement was self-evident, but it caused no end of attack. The president of the group said that my belief gave the young carte blanche to do anything they wanted. I tried unsuccessfully to get him to point out some effect that was bad in itself alone, but he couldn't grasp the idea that there is no cause in any effect.

Of course, that's understandable too. We are brainwashed from the time we are born to believe there is cause in effect. Every television show works on our minds with all the force of witchcraft. Commercials, designed to make us believe there is cause in some effect, say, "Take this pill . . . buy this deodorant . . . purchase this breakfast food," as though these effects will bring us closer to God, to our ultimate good. All of this world places its faith, hope, and trust in effects to protect us and to fulfill us. That belief itself is what this world is, the "this world" that Jesus overcame.

Nails, crosses, and swords were the most tempting effects of Jesus' day. If he had believed that they were cause, that they could kill, then he would not have risen from the cross. It doesn't even make any difference if you believe the stories that say Jesus wasn't actually dead, that he was just doped or nearly dead—still effects were not able to kill him, for they were not cause.

Don't forget for one second that everything created has been created by a cause. Things in themselves are not causes, and every time we fear an effect we are creating the "this world" belief that there are powers apart from God. When we see the world in terms of consciousness, when we know there is no cause in the visible scene, we are living in reality, and, what's more, we are still on earth. Consciousness may lead us to eat certain foods, take exercise, avoid poisons, but it is consciousness that is fulfilling us, not the foods; and the poisons, as effects, have no power to hurt us. Consciousness is God.

*Consciousness is my shepherd; I shall not want. Consciousness maketh me to lie down in green pastures: consciousness leadeth me beside the still waters. Consciousness restoreth my soul: consciousness leadeth me in the paths of righteousness (right identification) for his name's sake. Yea, though I walk through the valley of the shadow of death, I will fear no evil: for consciousness is with me. Consciousness is my rod and staff; they comfort me. Consciousness preparest a table before me in the presence of mine enemies (my ignorance). Consciousness anointest my head with oil; my cup runneth over. Surely goodness and mercy shall follow me all the days of my life: and I will dwell in the house of the Lord (in consciousness) forever.*

# THE
# SEARCH
# FOR SELF-LOVE

Sometimes, for brief moments, I love myself. That's the same as saying: Sometimes, for brief moments, I know myself. The rest of the time I am searching for my true identity, but that's nothing unusual or new. Even before Socrates told us there was nothing in the world more important than to "know thyself," every action man has taken, no matter how insignificant, has actually been related to his search for his true identity. I'm not talking only about the lofty pursuit of spiritual wisdom; even the most mundane day-to-day labors have been motivated by the desire to express the eternality we sense is our true nature. Even when a thief robs a bank, he is searching for a way to love himself. Instinctively he feels that to be powerful, rich, and strong would be his rightful place.

Obviously, then, everything at every level can be used to relate to our true identity—we should not be tempted to eliminate anything—and we can find ourselves anywhere we are at any moment.

That is why Jesus gave us the double thread commandment to love God and then, realizing that the second part was like unto the first, learn to love our neighbor as our selves. We've made a stab at the first half; now let's dig into the second. In a way, for now, the second is more important than the first because we are more familiar with personal sense, and the second commandment deals directly with personal sense, our own personal identity crisis.

Jesus said, "Love thy neighbor as *thyself*"; so there are again two parts that make up the one. We need to know how to love our neighbor in order to love ourselves, and we need to love ourselves in order to love our neighbor. It's impossible to do one without the other.

You've probably noticed that not only are we always asking ourselves who we are, but the first thing we do after meeting a stranger is to ask him who he is and where he has come from. Right away, we feel that perhaps if he knows who he is, we can relate and find out who we are.

We won't be able to know who either of us is without relativity, the capacity to comprehend clearly the man of earth self, and the man of God self, and then, after doing that, relate just where we are at any given moment. I promise you that if you can experience this ability you will be able to love at all times. After all, even Paul said, "We have a material body and a spiritual body." He didn't say we were two people; he said that although we are one person, we have two interpretations of self. He said we started out as spiritual, became material, and raised up the material into the spiritual once more.

Of course, I think Paul led us astray by an unfortunate choice of words. He labeled the natural man corrupt and the spiritual man incorrupt. The natural man is indeed at the level where perfection is not absolute, nor should be, but Paul laid a guilt trip on mankind by that language and defeated his own purpose. Certainly we put on immortality as mortality diminishes, and certainly our goal is to express pure immortality in order that, as Paul went on to say, "Death is swallowed up in victory," but this treasure hunt for immortality is the whole point of life, and if we believe the search is bad, then all life is bad.

For many years I fell for a mistake, which is incorporated in every teaching I have ever seen, until one day I stumbled on a clue which solved the problem and made it possible for me not to be guilty about my humanity. Every teaching I have come across implies that man was originally perfect, that man was in the Garden of Eden, in heaven, and that somehow he fell from grace and now has to return as though mankind was naughty. By implying man fell, we are made to feel guilty about being human.

The secret is this. Always first there is an idea, a concept, a truth, and *then* the idea becomes form or substance. An artist first gets an idea, and then later the idea is presented in form as a picture or a piece of sculpture. It isn't that the perfect form was there and somehow fell to pieces and has to be reassembled. First, the perfect form was just an idea, and it took time for the perfect idea to be expressed in perfect form. The perfect idea of man evolved in consciousness eons ago, and now we are growing closer each day to the perfect expression of that idea, but the time just hasn't come yet for this perfection to be expressed in the world of effects. That's why I have said that it is a sin to expect perfection. We are perfect, right now. We just haven't expressed our perfection perfectly in form. We'll get there, just give us a little time, but don't believe that we were once better than we are now.

I agree with the author James Leo Herlihy, who said, "Man is in the best shape he has ever been, and every man who ever existed could say the same thing." Every day we are evolving closer and closer to immortality; every day we are putting off incorruption. Everyone is doing the best he can at every moment. When we realize that, we take a big step forward in loving ourselves and our neighbors.

*Man did not fall. He is perfect idea in the process of becoming perfect form.*

Earlier in the book I mentioned an experience I had which was relevant to my personal struggle to match the idea to the form. I said I had just been through a "dark night of the soul." For a couple of years before I went through the experience I had a growing awareness that something, some sort of change or growth, was about to take place. I felt that I had to shed another skin, that I had to be pushed to a greater depth of awareness, that somehow my human self didn't fit *me*.

Everything in my outer life couldn't have looked better. Revelations were coming through meditation; healings and material fruits were plentiful. I was recognized as having achieved most of the goals of society and was accepted around the world by the spiritual family, but still I felt something was missing.

I didn't want to just stop. Ever since I had put my foot on the path I'd pushed on. When things would get too peaceful and I didn't think I was making progress I'd say, "OK, God, give me some more." Then when things got too rough I'd start to scream, "OK, that's enough. Stop! *Stop!*" I wanted to go all the way no matter what.

Finally I found myself out at the end of a limb. As far as human desires went there was nothing more I wanted, and that made life tough. As long as a person wants something he has a goal to head toward. But now, although I still enjoyed many of the human pleasures, there was nothing more at the material level I desired strongly enough to motivate me into that kind of trip.

I say there was nothing I wanted, and that isn't quite true. I wanted, and knew I wanted, more of the presence and feeling of my true self, of oneness with the source of being. So that's when it happened. I went into the darkness. Not only was I cut off from human feelings, but the one thing I wanted, that God feeling, totally departed.

There was no inner help, no voice, no direction. I was worse off than others because over the years I had come to depend entirely on my inner voice for direction. I called on everything I knew, tried every kind of prayer, studied all the clues I had discovered in the past, but nothing helped. I bathed myself in tears, some in pain, some in just plain self-pity.

I kept reminding myself that I had pointed out to others that downs were valuable and creative, that we should appreciate them and see what they had for us, but it didn't help. And to make matters worse, a number of my friends kept advising me to read my own books, that on page such and such I had said such and such—I wanted to throw the books at them. The gulf between my awareness and my ability to live by that awareness seemed insurmountable.

Ever since my first real contact in meditation some twenty-five years ago I would be frantic if I was unable to make contact for as long as a week or two, but this dark night lasted month after month. Finally it did its thing. It broke, and with it the veil was taken off. I saw what dark nights are all about and what their purpose is. I even saw that they are truly the gift of self.

For those of you who are not familiar with the term "dark night of the soul," let me explain. St. John of the Cross, a sixteenth-century Spanish monk-guide, wrote about an experience every seeker of the treasure undergoes at one time or another in one degree or another. He called it "the dark night of the soul," and he described its causes and purpose in order to help the young monks under his care through this jungle of spirit. His treatise was designed only for those who had committed themselves to finding the treasure, because he knew that those who were not on the path and hadn't realized moments of God contact wouldn't have the experience.

A dark night has two main purposes. The first is to purge the seeker of beliefs, old clues, old concepts, so that when the light returns, he can see his way free of past mistakes. Man with his mind starts assuming that the clues themselves are the treasure. As soon as a man believes he has faith, he is talking about theology, about concepts, but theology isn't God or self. Faith is something we *experience,* not something we *think.* A dark night beats a person to the ground until he loses faith in thinking, until his mind gives up and he experiences.

The other and most important reason for the dark night has to do with our brainwashing about who we are. Jung used the word "inflation" to explain it. He said that the distance between one's knowledge or concept of himself and one's personal development is the degree of his inflation. Often from studying with an advanced guide, from reading religious maps, or from valid personal inner revelation a seeker can discern truths intellectually way in advance of his own capacity to demonstrate these truths, thus bringing on a severe state of inflation.

Everyone has a degree of inflation. Everyone has a feeling of his true identity and a gap between that inner sense and his outer life, but extreme cases can be not only painful but even dangerous. Sooner or later, one has to catch up to the truths one has in his head, and a dark night is often how it happens.

A drug experience or repeated drug experiences can also bring on inflation. Sometimes through drugs a center of vision can be activated; a person sees more deeply into his true nature, but because the experience was not revealed in a natural way or by a guide, the clues are unrelated, and the gap between personal development and what was seen creates a desperate case of inflation. What is once experienced by drugs has to be reexperienced in a natural way without drugs in order to be real. Otherwise, it can make one more brainwashed than ever.

Today many of those who have been into the so-called drug culture may have induced an inflation that is leading up to a collective dark night. Though many are not monks in a monastery, they have shown by their life style and desires that they want to live spiritually. They have tried to follow all kinds of maps, having faith in each one, only to fail in the end. It has become harder and harder for them to keep their faith alight. They have no fruits to show for their journey and are beginning to despair. Of course, if the dark night leads them to a map that is right for them, if they find that there are no shortcuts, no quick easy way, that others can't make the trip for them, that they must make the trip themselves step by step, they will be way ahead and may be part of a mass awakening.

In order to help the young monks, St. John of the Cross also listed a number of things they could check on in themselves to see if they were building up to a dark night. For instance, they could check to see if they were growing in spiritual pride: the desire to speak of spiritual things in the presence of others, to want to teach spiritual things rather than learn or experience them themselves, to rush off and find a new guide when the old one points out faults, to make a public show of spiritual ecstasies and want to be noticed, to take the words out of the mouths of teachers as though one already knew them.

St. John also outlined other signs of impending spiritual indigestion under what he called spiritual avarice: not finding the consolation and satisfaction in spiritual things one would like to find, depending more and more on books rather than on action and doing for others, talking a good game but not working at it. He said that when a person dresses in a manner that implies he is following a spiritual life or makes a show of religious relics or burning incense unduly, his spiritual life is on the outside rather than on the inside.

St. John pointed out a subtle trick called the sin of luxury: overindulgence in the desire for feeling spiritual and the misuse of a natural gift for spiritual joy. Then there is the sin of wrath: becoming embittered and angry when delight and pleasure in spiritual things comes to an end, and turning to artificial stimulus in order to try to bring them back. There is impatience because the searcher isn't a saint in a day. There is switching from one kind of meditation to another when meditation no longer gives immediate pleasure, and finally, there is the resultant sloth which tempts one to abandon his own search.

All these missteps leading to the dark night are actually just the reverse side of virtues. No one ever gets to the treasure without having a tremendous hunger for spirit, without striving in every way to be spiritually aware, or without wanting his life to reflect his dedication, but when these virtues get misdirected a dark night comes.

Most of the stumbling blocks I just listed are found in the early part of the trip. I know. I experienced each of these myself at one time or another on my earlier trips. But as the trips go deeper, the clues become more subtle and are more easily mistaken. Believe me, no searcher or guide ever gets completely beyond taking wrong turns and paying the price. It's just that the later mistakes are of a different nature, and certain ones come only after deeper levels are touched.

The point is: we all face our misconception of who we are —none of us lives as relatively as we are meant to—so a dark night can come to all seekers, no matter how far on the path. By the dark night inflation is reduced, brainwashing is broken, and we can stand up face to face with our selves IN LOVE.

Inflation goes hand in hand with guilt, the wider the distance the greater the guilt, and guilt is the big spiritual "no-no." Guilt is the exact opposite of love; it is self-hate. We must eliminate guilt at every turn, or we will never find our selves. In fact, there would be no identity crisis at all without guilt.

If we take another look at our master map, the Bible, we find that the entire journey into darkness started with guilt. When the serpent tempted Eve it wasn't with an apple. Apples are merely effects, and as we just saw, effects are not cause; effects have no power. Look carefully at the words. The serpent said, "Eat of this fruit, and *then* ye shall be as the gods." In other words, the serpent implied: You are not good enough already. Eat of this fruit and you will be better. He made Eve feel guilty. The guilt he laid on Eve brought on her identity crisis. If she had known who she was and that she was already living in the kingdom of heaven she wouldn't have fallen for that temptation. In other words, she was tricked out of loving herself, and the minute she stopped knowing or loving herself, she got involved with the tree of the knowledge of good and evil and started the whole rat race of confusion.

The entire "this world" concept of life comes from the belief in good and bad. Good and bad are the entire substance of the false world. Good and bad create the belief that effects are cause. Every time we label something good or bad we create a wrong identification and are not loving.

Jesus exposed guilt and showed us a way out. For some delightful reason Jesus knew who he was. He really knew. He didn't quibble. He just stood up and said, "See me and you see my father." But he didn't deny he had human form. He also said, "Why callest thou me good?"—Why look at my body and try to put it under the illusion of bad and good? Why try to avoid seeing me as a whole person?

He showed that he had mastered the identity crisis because just after he attained his full illumination he was sent up into the wilderness, the wilderness of illusion or thought, and he, like Eve, was tempted. But he didn't fall for the trick. When Satan said, "*If* ye be the son of God, turn these stones into bread," Jesus just laughed and said, "Get thee behind me, Satan. I know who I am. I don't have to prove it. I have no guilt that makes me think I must appear Godlike, perfect, or all-powerful at this finite level."

In a way there is hardly a teacher in the world, myself included, who isn't a serpent laying guilt on others. The very minute I set forth a teaching, I am implying that you need to know yourself, that there is a state superior to the one you are in, and by doing that I engender potential guilt. It tempts you, like Eve, to think that if you eat of this apple, this teaching, you will be better. And certainly the minute a teacher walks around looking perfect, implying by dress or serenity that he has achieved a superior state, he is cramming guilt down another's throat. I suspect that those who huff and puff about their finite condition, those who constantly stumble over their clay feet, are more saintly than the teachers because they make you feel less guilty about your own shortcomings. In a way, I guess that is why we sometimes feel less guilty ourselves when we become aware of another's misfortunes—though we even start feeling guilty about that before long.

Before pursuing the search for self-love, let's explain another feeling many of us have had which has perhaps made us feel guilty because we didn't understand the underlying cause: that is the thought of suicide. We've been taught that suicide is a number one sin, yet which of us hasn't had thoughts of suicide at one time or another? In truth, the desire for suicide is a product of the identity crisis. The desire for suicide is the desire to get free from our inflation. We are not satisfied with our concept of who we think we are and want to eliminate it. Actually, no one commits suicide because he wants to die; he does it because he feels trapped in a false identity and wants to get out of the trap so he can live. Actual physical suicide is no answer because we are consciousness, not body, and we take our brainwashing right with us, only making it more real. But in spiritual terms Jesus commissioned us all to commit suicide. He said that we had to die daily, that we had to die to our brainwashed concept of who we were in order to have life eternal.

The desire for suicide is the finite self's impatience with its limitations. If one hadn't experienced the infinite potential within, if one hadn't experienced his divine nature, he wouldn't be impatient to express it, he wouldn't be willing to go to any extreme to grow. So go ahead, commit suicide, but do it the way Jesus instructed us: die to a false sense of self, die to a sense of guilt, and love yourself.

*Love is suicide to the ego.*

THE GOSPEL OF RELATIVITY

Now let's get down to business. Using our rule, first we examine the infinite side and then the finite.

> In my finiteness
> I'm a cork that's tossed on the sea,
> Unless somehow
> I can relate to infinity.

What is that infinity, that absolute to which I must relate in order to understand my finite nature? The clue to my infinite nature is: *I am invisible.*

I am invisible, and so are you. What people see is an effect. Our bodies are the result, the outer expression of consciousness. But we are consciousness, and no one sees consciousness; one can experience it, but not see it. I can be experienced but not be seen. I am CAUSE, not effect.

An automobile has a dual nature: it has a hidden motor that is the cause, that makes the auto run, and an outer covering that people see. I am the hidden cause. That, like the first commandment, is my greater self, the infinite unknowable. And that is invisible. You may think you know what is going on inside my body, inside my head, or in my consciousness, but you can't be sure, not really.

I am just as invisible to myself as I am to you. If I look in a mirror I don't see myself. I see the shell, the body of the automobile. I am that which is growing this person I call I. I am that which animates this body. I am that which makes my heart beat ("my" heart—I possess it, it is not me). I am that which makes my eyes see, my ears hear, my lungs breathe. As atoms come and go from this body daily, as old cells give way to new, I have many bodies, but I will always be here because I am the very life of this body, not the body alone. I have a body, I have intelligence, I have identity, I have talent, I have awareness, but I am not those things. I have them. I am life itself.

I am the "happening," the experience of life, the animating force, the "beingness" of myself. I have been told so long that I am a body that it is hard for me to realize I am that which is being the body, which animates it, which uses it. But I am the spirit of this body. I am spiritual. Just as Jesus said, "God is spirit," I am spirit, not form alone. I am that invisible immaterial life force which is the source of my awareness. God is invisible, and my nature is the same as God's.

All that we have just heard about the identity of God is true of my identity. All that God is "I AM," and all that "I" am God is.

As Jesus said, "Before Abraham was, I AM." I am eternal, I was never born, and I will never die. This body was born, but I have always been. I am perfect, flawless, total, and complete because I am the life of this body. This body will die, but I am life and cannot die.

I am conditionless being. What you see is conditioned and has age and identity, but I, the source of being, am conditionless. As Meister Eckhart cried, "A man should be as free of his own knowledge as when he did not exist. I pray God to rid me of God because conditionless being [being without any labels] is above God and above distinction. It was in this that I became myself and knew myself to make this man called 'I,' and I am my own cause. For this was I born. In my birth all things were born; if I had not been, then God could not have been either."

If I am not form, if I am conditionless being, if I am invisible, if I am that which is living this body, what am I? I am FUNCTION. If you really want to know who I am, figure out what my function is.

I'm not a "noun." I'm a "verb." There really aren't any nouns anyway, only verbs. When primitive man first used words there probably were no verbs; nouns themselves acted as verbs. He would say, "man," "fire," "water," meaning the function of man, the function of fire, the function of water.

A table isn't a table as such. It is consciousness functioning as table. If it couldn't be used as a table you couldn't call it a table. In that same way I am consciousness functioning as this body. Whatever function I perform in the world is what I am, not this body.

If I want to figure out what you mean to me I only have to ask myself what your function is in my life, and I am knowing you. If we conceive of the invisible nature of life we no longer think of a house as home, but home becomes a function. That's why the poets say that it takes more than a house to make a home. Everything has a function, and when we figure out what that is, we see the invisible nature or the reality. An automobile that doesn't work isn't an automobile. It's a pile of junk. A priest who doesn't show the power of love is not a priest. We will never be fooled or deceived if we look at the function, not the form, in order to know the truth. As Jesus said, "Ye shall know them by their fruits"—by their function.

*Use all your power of imagination. Think of yourself not as body but as that which is operating your body. Conceive of yourself as function.*

A good way to make a bridge into an understanding of our visible identity is to see our humanity as a pane of glass. Our absolute or invisible self is like pure light. If our visible identity is smudged with lots of dirt, not much light comes into the world, but if we are a clean glass the pure light comes in. Some people's identities are so muddied up that very little light shows forth, and everyone is painfully aware of their solid and obstructive personalities. Others approach the purity of Jesus, who was such a spotless windowpane that the pure light of his true self and the glass seemed one, not two.

Love, like light, finds its way into the world through individual beings, like windows to heaven. That's the only way light is going to come into "this world," through individuals. There isn't God and individuals. God or light will not come into the world unless there are enough pure panes of identity.

But here's the key, the key which eliminates guilt: the dirt on the pane is a fiction. It isn't real or permanent. If dirt or obstruction were the real nature of the person, it couldn't be changed or cleaned off. We, each one of us, really exist and have form. We are all panes of glass. We are real, potentially pure transparencies, and our false identity, our identity crisis, is temporary and unreal—it can be eliminated.

Each one of us since Eve has had to go through this cleansing identity crisis, for without each one of us there wouldn't be enough windows of love for the whole earth to be illuminated. Once full illumination is here there will be no more identity crisis for anyone.

When we say that someone has reached illumination it means simply that he, as Jesus, has reached the place where he is a pure transparency for his own true self to shine forth.

As I said earlier, when Paul said, "Have that mind which was in Christ Jesus," he meant have a transparent mind which reflects your pure God self. That's what repentance means. Whenever we realize we have been blocking the light, we have repented; we repent our not being transparencies for truth.

We have two identities at this third-dimensional level; one is our true self, and the other is our appearance. This was recognized when people referred to Jesus as the Christ. Jesus was the label they put on his form, and the Christ was the recognition of his invisible identity. It wouldn't be a bad idea if we went around doing the same thing with each other, if we said, "Hello, Mary Christ. Hello, Tom Christ. Hello, Walter Christ." That way we would be admitting the human identity and saluting the invisible one at the same time.

In our world identity, the whole man is made up of a body, mind, and expressed spirit. To know the human identity would be to know and experience the physical man, to experience his conscious mind, and to feel his personal spirit.

If I want to be a full and functioning human I must exercise and balance my body, mind, and spirit without giving any of the three sides the short end of the stick. I must learn to take my whole self into everything I do and learn how to keep from getting the parts of my human identity alienated or disconnected from the other parts. At any rate, man of earth is made up of body, mind, and spirit, but in order to see even that correctly we have to double think and not separate man into parts. Rather, we hold an awareness of the relativity of each of the parts as we study the whole. I should say rather that we are BODYMINDSPIRIT because the three make up the one human identity and shouldn't be separated.

A schoolteacher friend once told me that he found it necessary to give kids "wiggle room." He might have been talking about a physical condition, but all of us need wiggle room in terms of our identity. By freezing ourselves and others into one identity we are not only turning our back on relativity but we haven't begun to love in a practical way.

I evolved a wiggle room technique which has not only saved me lots of anguish and confusion but has made it possible for me to feel love as well as think it. I use an analogy based on the theater as a way of helping me let myself and others off the hook.

Our human identity is equated with the roles we play as actors on the stage. Our costume is our age, sex, profession, personality traits, the clothes we wear, our looks—everything in the physical world that identifies us. What appears to human sense is the part we play. That is all the audience, our associates, see. All the world ever recognizes is this false identity.

Back in the dressing room, "in the secret place of the most high," we are not in costume and the true us is revealed. We stand in our full glory as sons of God, perfect and unconditioned. Very, very few ever see us in that state; the price is too high. The key to the dressing room is love, the ability to *know* us as we are.

Now, the world, "this world," is the stage set. When we look at it at face value we are seeing a facsimile, an *imitation* of reality made up of canvas, paint, and optical illusion.

Our problem is that we confuse the set and the parts the actors are playing with reality. As long as we are on earth we are in the theater (as Shakespeare said, "All the world's a stage"), but that doesn't mean we have to be fooled into believing that what we see with our eyes is the truth of life. The degree we believe that what we see is reality is the degree of our brainwashing.

What we have to do to be free is double think. We have to see the drama without falling for a belief that there is a power apart from God's, without believing that the actors themselves are really going to die, and we have to remember that the actor on the stage is not really the person he appears as. In other words, the actor can't be blamed for the actions the playwright (universal ignorance) had him perform.

We don't ignore either side. We see the stage set, we see the actors, and we know that they exist at the level of "this world," but we double think and know at the same time that what we see is not total reality—it's relative. Then we are free to forgive and to love.

For that matter, this is how we love *ourselves*. We are all playing parts, and if we take them too seriously, if we forget that we are acting, we get in trouble.

Sarah Bernhardt, one of the world's greatest actresses, was once watching a performance from off stage. A young actress was playing her part with such emotion that the tears streamed down her face. She had forgotten she was acting and had become the part she was playing. When the young actress left the stage Bernhardt stopped her and with guru-like wisdom said, "When you cry the audience doesn't." In other words: when you get the actor and the part you are playing confused and lose the double thread you are not effective—you fail. As every athlete knows, tighten up and you miss the ball.

The lives we live are the roles we play like parts an actor plays in a stock company. One week we play Hamlet, one week Othello, one week Macbeth. We are not any of these parts ourselves. That's why it is tricky to say, "In my last incarnation I was a priest" or "I was Cleopatra." *You* were none of those people. You are only the Christ. You might have appeared in some of those roles, but God is the only truth of your permanent identity.

In the same way, when astrologers tell you about your chart, or when people psychoanalyze you (or when you play amateur psychologist and analyze others), remember that their conclusions apply to the part you are playing, not you. Don't mistakenly put yourself under the limitations of those laws by believing they are talking about the real you. If you do you are not loving yourself.

Certainly, we want to play the part we have been given as well as possible; so we can use astrology, psychiatry, or the *I Ching* to help us understand the part, but we must watch out that we don't lose sense of our true identity. The important thing to remember is that all the roles —Hamlet, Macbeth, Othello—are fictions invented by a playwright. Although they have no actual reality, they do have value. We all need parts to play on the stage, and our roles help us grow and entertain others, but we must realize that our human identity is only a fiction.

This theater analogy can really be a help because at any moment it can make it possible for us to forgive ourselves and others. At any moment we can stop and observe the self. We can forgive those around us by recognizing the difference between their true being and their act. That's love.

# THE
# PRACTICE
# OF BEING

We are getting closer to the treasure than you might think. The only thing that hides it now is the magic, the experience. With the two commandments we have been establishing the two foundation corners of a kind of trinity. Now we are ready to apply these principles to create a third element: the experience.

The principle of the trinity, whether symbolized in the advent of Jesus or as a principle that applies to all creativity, is simple, but yet it is one of the most esoteric secrets of life. Unfortunately, in the Christian world, it was believed that the trinity related only to Jesus, and we failed to see it as the principle behind all creativity.

Let's look at the Trinity. One aspect is "the Father," the fathering principle, the absolute, the power. The second aspect is "the Son," the visible, finite expression, the word made flesh, the individual. These two are the double thread. Both are needed, just as a boy scout needs both flint and metal to make fire. Only when the two are brought together does creativity take place. Creativity, the third aspect, is the equivalent of the Holy Ghost, the spirit, the fire, the happening, the thing that creates.

The happening is freedom itself—it's the treasure. If we don't succeed in achieving it our whole trip is a failure. We want to make fire; the love of God is like the flint, and the love of neighbor is like the metal surface on which the flint is struck. When the two are brought together by right action, we have a spark of life.

This trinity principle applies in every area of life, in everything creative we do. In art, half the job is collecting our paints, brushes, and materials. Then we bring our talent and creative intention to bear. Hopefully the creative spark is struck when these two are combined. The result is something new and beautiful.

In creating myself, as well, my two I's meet: the "I" Walter strikes up against the "I" Christ, and growth takes place. I don't want to lose sight of either "I" until I am fully grown.

Jung said that only at the material level can growth take place, and then only by a combination of the forces of spirit and matter. After death, he claimed, there is no growth because materiality is needed to fuel growth. Teilhard had a similar thesis.

But here right action comes in. We have to know how to combine the elements. A number of religions have so feared any action at all that they have ended up teaching people to do nothing, to try to avoid life. This accomplished exactly what they set in motion—nothing. No, worse than that—by cutting off action, they have destroyed what had been created before. A man is made to create, and if he isn't creating he isn't healthy.

Man is potentially a conversion machine designed to convert spirit into matter. Man is different from other animals because he can create new forms, not just instinctively create nests and so on. He can do this because he has an invisible spirit within him, God. We say man is made in the image of God, because we know that God is creativity and man is made in that image.

Just as an automobile isn't healthy if it isn't running on all its cylinders, a man isn't healthy if he isn't running on all of his, if he isn't creative. Man is designed with a daily flow of creative energy, and he must give vent to this energy. Just as he is designed to eliminate physical energy and waste materials every day, he is designed to use his creative energy daily. Those who sit around creating nothing at all, taking but not giving, get depressed. They're sick.

Certainly, there are times when it is necessary to go on retreats in order to store up energy in preparation for some act which will make the world a better place, but after a while the energy we have stored up must be spent, or we cease to function as a whole person. On the other hand, the Victorian belief that we should feel guilty if we are not working every minute is the reverse of doing nothing and must also be avoided. Again, it is all a matter of relativity. What we must watch out for is the impulse to O.D., to overdose, on trying to create too much or too little.

Today the pendulum of life swings to such extreme ends that many O.D. on everything they do or take. We have become chronic O.D.'ers because we have not grasped the secret of the double thread, of balance, and because we haven't realized that the only way we can keep check to see if we are O.D.-ing is to get quiet and meditate. Meditation is needed to show us the relative situation.

It is easy to understand why we are tempted to O.D. At the unconscious level we all realize that our true identity is infinity, that we should have access to all the heavenly riches or heavenly pleasures; so we don't stop with a taste —we want the whole pie. The urge to O.D. is really a manifestation of the urge to demonstrate our infinity. We curb it only by realizing that because of our oneness with God we already have access to infinity.

Many of us O.D. on religion, and that is far more harmful than O.D.-ing on eating or drinking. Too much knowledge sets up inflation and a widening imbalance between our two realities. This, in turn, makes living by relativity impossible. The remarkable thing is that too much knowledge is more harmful than too little. Most of us have too big a gap between our spiritual knowledge and our ability to apply it. We have to start loving ourselves enough to just "be," and to stop widening the gap between where we think we'd *like* to be and where we *are*.

*It's healthy to have our focus a bit ahead of ourselves—we need to aim at something—but let's coordinate our actions with our awareness, aim at the NEXT possible step, and not O.D.*

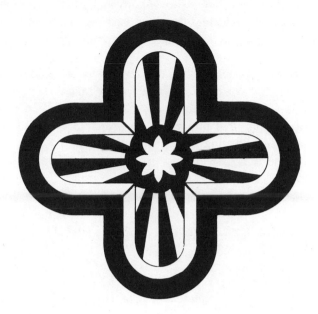

Right action is based on two steps (our two commandments): first, we get quiet in order to receive right instructions; second, we act on the instructions we receive. But it is surprising how few people can really grasp that. Not long ago I gave a talk at Stanford University. On the platform with me were two students, a militant student body officer and a theology student, who were to make comments after I spoke. That was fine with me. I talked the double thread message, and I thought I'd gone over the double aspect enough to answer any queries, but the whole time I was talking both students were so busy taking notes that they couldn't hear. When I finished, the militant student said, "You have a perfectly selfish philosophy. You talk about going within, but there are people in the ghettos who need to be fed . . . ," and so on. I rebutted by reminding him that I had said we were not loving our neighbor if we didn't do two things: know the true identity of our neighbor and take action to aid him materially. Then I asked the student why he was in college. He answered that he was there to learn about life from the people he encountered and from his teachers in order to be able to make a better world. So I pointed out to him that he was doing just what I said: he was getting his tools together in preparation for using them.

After he finished with me, the theology student spoke up. He too said, "You have a perfectly selfish religion. You leave God out. You talk about going within yourself." So I had to remind him that in a changing world if I did not relate to some unchanging absolute truths, I had no direction, and those truths were God. I had to know God for right action.

One of the main reasons we have not known how to act is because religions imply that heaven is other than *here* and *now,* that heaven is off in the here and after. In most religions heaven isn't "here" and "now"—it's "there" and "then."

Today we hear a lot about the *here* and *now,* about people attempting to live in the here and now without much success. That's because the here and now are only half the truth. Like the trinity, the here and now need a third aspect —WHEN. "When" is the spark.

The Bible says that evils will not come nigh your door *when* you live in the secret place of the most high—when you identify correctly. Jesus said, "Ye shall know the truth, and the truth shall make you free"—*when* you know it. The complement to here and now is "when."

We see lots of people today who have dropped out of society, who have understandably migrated to warm pleasant places in order to have a good here and now. They lie on the beach baking like turtles all day, innocently thinking that they are in right action because they are trying to be in the "here" and "now." I was discussing this with Lama Govinda not long ago, and he said, "The trouble is that they don't realize living in the here and now means living in the *eternal* here and the *eternal* now—not in a hedonistic or materialistic concept of here and now."

Remember that everything we see is not what we see with our eyes; it is actually consciousness expressing itself in form. You are not a body; you have a body. And since time is not real, the now is not a matter of time—it's a matter of *spirit,* the spirit you are in.

If we are not already there, how do we get into an eternal

sense of here and now? Of course, I think meditation is the way. Meditation is always the foundation of right action. We take our directions from meditation before we act. Meditation is the great gift of the Orient. Meditation is the HOW, the vertical relativity of man to God. The Christian map revealed the WHAT, what we are to accomplish, the word made flesh, the lateral relativity of man to man. So when we put the "how" and the "what" together and experience the spark, we have right action.

When I tell you to get in the "here" and "now" by meditating, it's rather like the conductor of an orchestra tapping his baton to gain the attention of the musicians. He is saying: Everybody get in the here and now, get quiet, tune in with one another. But the conductor doesn't stop there. After he has the orchestra's attention, he gives them the signal to start making music. There's no point in getting centered if you don't intend playing.

On the other hand, we in the Occident believe in playing. We are great at getting things done, but because we have not started by getting centered, by getting into the here and now, we are all playing different tunes, and there is chaos, inharmony, and destruction. In the Orient, many spend time leaving the world of appearances and going within, but they don't use what they find there as a springboard to action, and they make no music.

> *When the East meets the West, or vice versa,*
> *HERE and NOW will be combined with WHEN*
> *and the music of the spheres will lift the world into*
> *the light.*

As I said, "now" is a matter of spirit; so almost the first practical-action clue we should remember is always to start by checking where our spirit is, the spirit in which we act. The Christian message tells us to spread "glad tidings." Whenever one calls himself a follower of Christ and for one second preaches bad tidings, evil and negatives, he is kidding himself. We have to act, but *never* from the level of bad tidings.

The first words Jesus spoke after he had been Christed and

returned from overcoming the temptations were a quote from Isaiah 61: "The spirit of the Lord God [the absolute] is upon me; because the Lord hath anointed me to preach good tidings unto the meek; he hath sent me to bind up the brokenhearted, to proclaim liberty to the captives, and the opening of the prison to them that are bound." Through this, he said, we "shall build the old wastes, shall raise up the former desolations, and shall repair the waste cities, the desolations of many generations." First, get into the spirit, then preach glad tidings, and the result will be freedom for mankind from his prisons of lack, limitation, ill health, and all the destructions of the past.

The key word is "spirit." It's this simple—*when the spirit in which you do things is more important than the results, you are spiritual.* When the results are more important than how you go about getting them, you are lost in the world of effect and doomed to failure. Right action pursues spirit before results. It really means that we should never, but never, do anything if we can't do it in the right spirit. That's living Godly, spirit-ually.

The right spirit behind our action is vitally important for another reason. Christian theology has a fancy word for it, eschatology. Eschatology means that there is an inherent hope in the Christian message—that at the end we can have freedom from death. That belief is the cornerstone because it gives mankind hope. Without hope man can't move. Modern cynical philosophies which reduce man to the level of helpless animals fool themselves. Without hope it's impossible to create. No artist would ever try to create if he didn't have hope that he could do it, hope that from the invisible he could bring something into the visible. The appeal of art is its inherent hope. When we stand before a work of art we feel free and good because we subconsciously realize that another person created the work of art, which shows man can transcend material limitations, and we, being humans ourselves, can potentially do the same thing. Art is hope-full.

Hope is the greatest gift we can be given, and the greatest thing we can do for anyone else is to give him hope, even if it makes no logical sense to do so. Crepe hangers who feel that the world is getting worse and worse and that doom is around the corner are stabbing their fellow man in the back, for without hope, life is not worth living.

That's why we must be sure people know what the eternal here and now really are. If a person thinks that the here and now are the "this world" dog-eat-dog sense of life, he loses hope because his life isn't always too pleasant, but if he knows that hopefully he can find the real here and now, he has a reason to keep trying.

Look at your own self: there have been times when you could hardly get up off the ground. Advice didn't help. When people pointed out your faults that only made things worse. But along came some friend who said something or did something that gave you some hope. It didn't make any difference if he was impractical and off in space. When you became hopeful you began to move—and when you moved, grace began to flow once more and your spirit came alive.

*I am truly a spiritual being when the spirit in which I act is more important than the results I set out to achieve. When my being radiates hope my spirit is love.*

The next clue is one we have touched on many times already. It not only proves why we must put spirit first at all times, but it is the key to all right action. I wanted to start the whole map with this clue, just as the apostle John started his map, the Gospel of St. John, with it, but I was afraid it wouldn't be understood without all the other clues. Let's take a look at John's words, go through them, and then decipher them step by step.

*In the beginning was the Word, and the Word was with God, and the Word was God. The same was in the beginning with God. All things were made by him; and without him was not anything made that was made. In him was life; and the life was the light of men. And the light shineth in darkness; and the darkness comprehended it not.*

In the beginning (at the start of every thing or action) is a WORD, an IDEA, a THOUGHT. This original word or idea is not only with God—it actually *is* God. The word creates. Ideas create. So ideas and words are the creative principle which is God. God is not a thing or person; it is conscious-ness. The word represents consciousness.

All things, John tells us, are made by consciousness, and not a single thing has been made any other way. He goes on to say that the world, man's ignorance, can't understand this, although the light shineth in the darkness. The world won't accept this clue, just as the world won't accept that there is no cause in effect, that material things are not cause. *Spirit is the substance of all form.*

When we see forms we are seeing ideas. The invisible idea is the cause and the reality. There really isn't any differ-ence between the idea and the form. John was telling us how to love, how to identify—spirit is the true identity of every person or thing.

Sometimes I have said that I don't see people, and others have thought I was ready for the booby hatch. Well, to "this world" sense, I was, but in truth I wasn't just talking. Natu-rally I see forms; I see bodies and people. But when I see a person I am more aware of his consciousness than the form. I am more aware of the cause than of the effect. I see both, but I know which is the greater reality. In the beginning was a consciousness, a philosophy, an attitude or spirit, and this resulted in a visible form; but first was the idea.

All forms are just the *symbols* of consciousness. In fact, everything you see in the world of form is *symbolic*. Even your own body is a symbol, the symbol of your body consciousness. As humans we confuse the symbols with the things they symbolize; so with this clue in mind, we can reverse things and see all effects as the symbols of consciousness. Man is spiritual. What we see is the symbol of that spirit.

Everything appearing in the world is the word, consciousness, formed, so if I expect to live by right action I must constantly watch my own consciousness, which is constantly at work creating. We can know we are acting rightly at all times if we identify rightly at all times, knowing that *God is the consciousness of all form.* When we are loving, we know that there is nothing but God. When all we see is God, the forms match our vision.

When Paul said, "God is not mocked," he was right. We can't cheat. Our life is a reflection in form of our own consciousnesses. We can't mock that principle. We can't hide behind the barn and say two times two is five and get away with it. Creative truth follows us everywhere, and if the word or idea in our heads is wrong the forms turn out to match.

If we want to change our lives and even alter the material things we see in our lives, there is *only* one way. We have to change our own consciousnesses, because our consciousness creates our lives.

The first law of spiritual living is: we are never dealing with persons, places, things, or situations but rather with our concepts of that which appears. We must go within our own consciousness and resolve all appearances. That means that we can never blame anyone or anything in the visible world because we know that our whole life is the result of our own consciousness. This leaves us nowhere to hide. But it is also great because we are the masters of our own lives, and we have the power to change ourselves.

We create ourselves when we have the right idea or word in our consciousnesses. That's what prayer is: entertaining the truth in consciousness. Prayer is idea expressing itself. So often those who don't realize that the word becomes flesh find themselves doing the opposite of what they wish. They reinforce the negative. When they pray to get over depression, to eliminate fear, loneliness, or lack, they create those conditions by giving them power in thought. When prayer is a positive acceptance that God already IS, when prayer is a vision of harmony already existing, when prayer is the realization that *God is the true substance of all form,* then the word is made flesh.

Whenever we try to change the human picture, the world of effects, we are actually sitting in judgment and reinforcing the illusion. Remember, *God is not in the human scene.* The human scene is a false sense of what really is. As long as we try to find God in that illusory world we are bound to lose faith; as long as we brag about appearances, we are looking for God in the wrong place. Right action is to remove our eyes from materialistic judgments for a while, go within the invisible, and establish ourselves in the right word or spirit where "my kingdom" exists, and then, paradoxically, the kingdom is created and appears outwardly.

A passage in the book of Isaiah says, "Cease ye from man, whose breath is in his nostrils: for wherein is he to be accounted of?" which is like saying that when we are dealing with individuals God is not in the human scene. Man, whose breath is in his nostrils, is the actor on the stage and no amount of thinking or logic can help understand that character. When the problem is to understand another human being in a spiritual sense, we do it by refusing to become psychoanalysts and making no attempt to understand the person with our minds. This way we make it possible for the Christ self to appear.

In other words, no matter how impossible or confusing it seems to our rational minds, the essential principle for right action is: *never try to change the human picture.* Take action, lots of action, but take creative action, not action designed to fiddle with the human or false picture.

That is a principle that needs to be complemented by an additional clue which, together with the previous one, creates the kingdom of heaven on earth: *have God and you have all.* The word is God and the word gives rise to all form. When you have God you have all. We don't have to go to God for health, for wealth, for companionship, for anything. God is the *only* cause. When we have God we have all the things we want. Because God is omniscient, we don't even have to inform God of our needs; we only have to make

God contact, and the contact forms whatever it is we need.

I know this takes double think, but the truth is that God IS literally peace itself, God IS health, God IS companionship, God IS joy, God IS supply, God IS harmony. God actually IS all of these things; if you have God, you are bound to have these as well.

*In the beginning is the word. This word is God, and my life is God-life expressing itself when I no longer try to change the human picture, cease from man whose breath is in his nostrils, and let the word fill my consciousness.*

The symbol of the Christian message is the cross. When I was a kid I used to hear people say, "Have you accepted the cross?" and it made me want to throw up. It was said in such a way as to imply: Have you accepted pain and suffering as the way of life? The cross seemed to symbolize pain and anguish; so I certainly didn't want that symbol hanging around my neck.

Now I realize that the old interpretation is exactly the opposite of the true symbolism of the cross. "Have you accepted the cross?" really means: Have you accepted the fact that Jesus got off the cross? If you believe he did survive the cross, then you believe that spirit triumphs over matter, that *there is no cause in effect.* If Jesus got off the cross, the cross symbolizes freedom from materiality. The cross represents the glad tidings of the Christian message. It symbolizes Christ-consciousness.

In the highest sense, to accept the cross, or to accept Jesus, is to accept that what was true of him is true of you yourself. It is no good to see the cross as a unique experience for one man alone. Unless we realize that the truth of Jesus is alive because it is the truth of ourselves, we have neither accepted the cross nor Jesus—nor ourselves. When someone asks you if you have accepted Jesus, smile, say "yes," and know you are accepting the same freedom for yourself.

Sometimes I hear people talk about the antichrist, and I am not sure just what they mean. But to me the antichrist would have to be anything opposite to the meaning of the cross or the Christ. In other words, anyone who believes there is cause in effect would have to be antichrist.

Or it could be put this way: anyone who believes that effects have power, who puts his faith and trust in effects, is on the side of the antichrist. Any government, organization, profession, or person who believes that a society can be chemically tranquilized into heaven, or that material means can solve man's problems, is tricked into the antichrist.

But my concern isn't with trying to change other people. That would be trying to change the human picture; that would be believing in a power apart from God's. My concern is about my own right action, about how I can keep from being tricked by the antichrist myself. And there is a guideline I follow which is just about the most helpful clue to right living I know. In fact, it is the clue that more than any other brought me out of my dark night experience and gave me something to lean on until my inner spirit once more directed my life.

This clue is a combination of two statements from the Bible: "Choose you this day whom ye will serve," and "ye cannot serve God and mammon." God is spirit, the inner reality, and mammon represents everything in the world of effects. Mammon isn't just money and materiality. Mammon represents everything that can be named, labeled, or defined. All teachings, all philosophies, all systems, all thoughts, all techniques or methods, are mammon. That means that whenever we serve a particular teaching, some ethic, or some system of thought, as well as when we serve material things, we are serving mammon.

The operative word in this clue is the word "serve." "Choose you this day whom ye will *serve,* God or mammon." That doesn't mean that we can't *use* mammon. It means we should choose whether we want to use mammon or *serve* it. It says we should serve God and use mammon.

Unfortunately, most people serve mammon and try to use God to get more of it. Mammon is fine, it's a blessing and it's there to be enjoyed, but we, if we want to be on the side of the Christ, must serve God the invisible creative spirit and use the effects.

As soon as we begin to care too much about any way of thinking, any system of philosophy, any medicine or food, we are serving something other than God; so at one time or another we have to choose to live by spirit and check to see what we are serving. We do this by fasting.

Anytime we feel that we are becoming dependent on some form of mammon we can set a period of fast long enough to break its power over us and return to serving God. Once we really demonstrate to ourselves that we can stop serving whatever form of mammon it is that tricks us, we will never again be in bondage to that form.

To fast is to abstain from something for a while, and Jesus said in reference to particularly difficult problems, "This one goes not out except by prayer and fasting." He didn't necessarily mean fasting from food. Any time we give something up for a period we are fasting. Sunday is a fast from the work of the week. Sleep is a fast from activity. But we can learn a lot from using a food fast as an example.

The true purpose of a fast is to remove one from the law of mammon. Many have an instinctive desire to fast, but by not realizing the true purpose, they simply remove themselves from one law and place themselves under another law. Many fast to get out from under the law of meat and potatoes and end by putting themselves under the law of fruit and nuts. I must admit that the law of fruit and nuts is a better law to live by than the one of meat and potatoes, but it is still living by the law and giving power to effects. Fruit and nuts are just as much effects as meat and potatoes. Law means living by effects, either bad ones or good ones.

The man "who has his being in Christ" is one who lives by grace rather than law. He has a diet to live by, and it's the most strict diet of all, but it isn't a diet which gives power to food or effects. His diet is to eat what his inner spirit tells him to eat. He goes within, gets quiet, listens to his inner direction, and eats what it tells him to. The tricky thing is that his inner guidance will most likely tell him to eat pure food, to avoid poisonous things, to eat little meat. As I said before, his inner voice will instruct him in the relative balance between the Yin and Yang. A true diet is the diet of spirit, not effect. After one is out from under bad and good, or law, when it is necessary to eat a bit of meat one will not suffer ill effects because he isn't under the law of body.

The people who are going to survive in the future will be those who have come out from under the laws of such effects as DDT and bad air. Survival won't be found by those who think that they have to go where the effects are good, where there is no DDT or pollution. The belief that Jesus survived the cross is the belief that man can come out from under the law of effect, and we do that by breaking the law through fasting mentally from the thoughts that give power to effect, from fasting physically by rejecting the control of effects, and from fasting from negative spirit no matter what our minds try to tell us.

Law is a jail warden, but it also can make us free. As long as we know that law exists only on the stage, at the third-dimensional level, we can use it rather than it us. For every human law there is always another law which breaks it.

Remember, we must choose. And we must never let anyone or anything have our choice, because no one can know what is going on inside of us; no one can know where we are in the scheme of relativity. Not even the greatest guru can know completely where we are individually. Everyone must walk the last mile alone. A guru can lead us lovingly up to the last mile, to our choice, to our free will, but we have to make that walk ourselves, and we can do it by choosing which we will serve, God or mammon.

*This moment can be the turning point in my whole life if I resolve this moment to choose the Christ, to choose to serve cause, to serve God.*

One last step. The Bible says, "The last enemy that shall be destroyed is death." This is the big one. All the other little laws just lead to this one. We can come out from under all the laws of effect. We can no longer need eight hours of sleep a night, no longer need vitamin supplements, no longer be under the law of lack or any of the many, many laws we have been duped into accepting. It all adds up to the same thing: we must come out from under *all* law.

Paul put it in another way: "Without the law sin was dead. For I was alive without the law once: but when the commandment [laws] came, sin revived, and I died. And the commandment, which was ordained to life, I found to be unto death." When we fell for the belief that there were moral and physical laws we should live by, we actually bought death.

What do we do? If we resist evil we only create more of it. If we fight the law we give it power. We do what Jesus told us to do: *"Agree with thine adversary."*

When I first came across this clue I couldn't have been more confused. I had always thought I was supposed to stand up for right. I thought I was supposed to work without ceasing to be a better person and not fall for ignorance. Now

Jesus was telling me to agree with my adversary. Finally other clues came to my rescue, and I saw the light.

If "my kingdom is not of this world" where there is cause in effect, and if I choose spirit rather than mammon, then there is nothing to resist. Agreeing with my adversary means: "let go," "let be," SURRENDER.

There it is, the most difficult clue of all—surrender. The only flag to fly is the white flag of surrender, for when we resist *any* evil, in our selves or in others, we create law.

Many of us want to surrender without even knowing it. That's why we play music that is so loud and strong in vibration that the only thing we can do is surrender to it. Many have been attracted to drugs because they want to surrender. When a person takes a drug he has surrendered himself. But now we must surrender to the only thing worthy of surrender—our selves, our true being, God.

The antichrist ignorance afoot in the world has been called the "black brotherhood," the brotherhood of ignorance. That force can seem very real and apparent at times, and many are tempted to fight it. But there is only one way to overcome the ignorance in the world: surrender. The only power the forces of ignorance have is the power we give to them by our fears and resistance. When we agree with our adversary by total faith, total surrender, all false powers have nothing more to sustain them.

The secret is we must die to live. We must surrender in order to attain all we have sought by struggle. We must love ourselves enough to dare to surrender. Consciously stop. Consciously give up. Consciously seek no further.

Consciously surrender your body, healthy or unhealthy. Consciously surrender your mind, all you have learned and all you have not learned, all old knowledge and all new. Consciously surrender your spirit, your high spirit or your low spirit.

Surrender your desire to be anything more than what you are, surrender your desire to be anywhere other than where you are, surrender your desire to have more of God in your life.

*SURRENDER*

# THE
# PASSWORD

The light shines. This is the day of ascension. Time is ended. There was a time in my life, in your life, and in the life of the world when we experienced the Holy Week. We experienced the crucifixion—action, law, the material death. We celebrated the crucifixion; we exalted Jesus as a body on the cross. Then we experienced the resurrection—spirit, prayer, healing, grace, and truth. We celebrated a power that healed, lifted, and triumphed over the material. Now we are ready to celebrate a new Easter, the ascension. No longer will Easter be crucifixion and resurrection without the crowning glory, the spark brought about through the crucifixion and resurrection—the ascension of consciousness, total oneness.

We have experienced many crucifixions and many resurrections, almost daily, but there is only one ascension. Once the consciousness breaks through to the secret, it never turns back. Like a flower blossoming, it never retreats into the bud.

Each of these crucifixions has been an initiation. All experience in human awareness is only symbolic of the initiation of our consciousness into our final anointment as priests of life. Every hardship, every death, every experience has been an initiation. We have heard of the mystical initiations through which the masters of old led their students and have not realized that everything we have thought of as our human experience has been our initiation.

Initiations are minor deaths leading to the final death of our false sense of self. First, the initiate is led to a fiery pit and is told he must walk through it. In order to continue he has to die to his fear, but if he does, he experiences the first miracle—the fire does not burn. Next he is led to a door through which he must pass. He opens the door and finds a pit of snakes. Once more he is called on to die to his material sense of self, and he finds as he passes over the pit that the snakes have no power—their bites cannot pain or kill. On and on the initiate passes through the full catalog of human experience as each of us does. Every temptation, every death, every fear, is a ritual of initiation. Finally at the very end when the initiate thinks he is beyond all caring he is led to a high cliff. Below the cliff the rocks appear to be strewn with the crushed bodies of those who have fallen. The masters say, "Jump. We leave you here. You must go the last mile alone." If the initiate cannot experience this aloneness of spirit, aloneness of mind, and aloneness of body he turns back and never realizes that the initiation is all a dream. If he jumps, it is his final act of surrender and faith. He jumps because he feels the love of the masters. He knows they are there and they have been initiated themselves; so he jumps. And when he jumps he awakens in the everlasting arms. Free, pure, light.

He is no longer confused by Jesus' statement, "Follow me, my burden is light." Before, when he had heard that statement he was confused because Jesus' burden of scorn and crucifixion had seemed heavy, very heavy, too heavy. Now he knows that Jesus' burden was not lightweight. His burden was THE LIGHT. Light itself. Now the initiate realizes that the closer he gets to the light the greater burden it becomes to reflect the light into darkness. His burden, the light, has been his blessing and his trial.

Now he sees that Jesus' life was an explanation of the initiation which each and every spiritual being must undergo. He experiences the anguish of self-doubt that Jesus suffered in his Gethsemane initiation, where he was tempted to believe he led his followers astray, where he was tempted to believe he had failed, that he couldn't take it.

And finally the greatest of all initiations, *the cross.* He sees that on the cross Jesus finally gave up. Never before the cross had he completely given up. Always before he had felt that if he healed, taught, and helped God he would be earning his position as the son of God. When he finally gave up and cried out, "Why have you forsaken me?" he gave up believing he could earn his sonship and he "let" God, not himself, resurrect him.

On the cross Jesus stopped looking for proof. He stopped saying, as we have so often, that he would love God *if* God raised up his body. When he stopped looking for proof, surrender was complete, and he not only came off the cross but he ascended into pure consciousness, all trace of self merged into Self.

The Christ-consciousness IS God. There is no other God. Having attained Christ-consciousness, Jesus was God. God, Christ-consciousness, did not send Jesus; it was expressed in the flesh *as* Jesus.

Christ consciousness IS. When I surrender to Christ-consciousness, I am God. There is no God and. . . . Now I know when I see Jesus, when I see myself, when I see you, I see God because he is Christ-consciousness. Christ-consciousness exists today; so Jesus exists today. There is no unformed consciousness; so Jesus exists today in form. When I let Jesus into my heart I let Christ-consciousness into my heart, and the form of Jesus is MY form. I am Jesus. For I have dared to voice the secret of all secrets, the password—"I."

From the beginning of time the password has been kept secret. Those who have tried to use the word carelessly have been thrown into darkness. It must be kept secret and sacred always. It must never, never be shared with those who are unprepared, because it will utterly destroy them.

There is no other password, not another. This password is the same over the entire world, through all of history. It was the word spoken by the priests of Atlantis, it was Melchizedek's secret, it was the password of master craftsmen, the masons who built the pyramids, and when it was misused it destroyed Atlantis, it lost the secret of the pyramids, and it blinded mankind.

When Jesus tried to tell the password he said, "There is only one way you can enter the kingdom." He said, "I AM the way," but mankind didn't hear. They thought he was saying that Jesus, the man, was the way, but he was saying the password, "I."

That's it. That's all. Just "I." So simple, but so very, very complicated. For "I" cannot be spoken; it can be felt and experienced, but not thought. Any thought about "I" carries with it the seeds of ego, separation, and defeat. "I" is the most sacred of all words because it can be comprehended only in silence, in an inner silence.

We have missed the secret of life because we have spoken it. In fact, we have spoken it more than any other word, and every time we have said "I" in a finite way we have desecrated the word. Whenever we have said, "I feel depressed" or "I feel sick," "I need this" or "I need that," we have closed the door on ourselves. We have misused the password.

Whenever we have called any man on earth our father, any guru, any mate, any effect, we have shut the door on "I." Those who know I AM will never have to look to man whose breath is in his nostrils for anything. They can travel anywhere in the world without money or protection. Everything will be provided from the "I" within.

But we must not speak "I." We must hear it. "I" must enter the heart, it must be in the soul, it must be felt rather than reasoned or thought; only then do we dwell in the secret place of the most high. And it says to us, "Know ye not that *I* am God? 'Be still and know that *I* am God.' *I* in the midst of you is mighty, and *I* will never leave you, nor forsake you.

"*I* am Melchizedek. *I* am he that was never born and will never die, self-complete. *I* am the offspring of God, God itself appearing in form, God appearing as my own individual being."

Say "I." Say it to yourself. Realize that it is the one thing every man in the world has in common—everyone can say "I." Everyone can use the password. Surrender to the realization that your "I" has been the only life you have really ever had or ever will have, and that isn't apart from you; it is right where you are. There is nothing religious or spiritual about the password. It just is, and it is the only reality.

*I* in the midst of me feeds me, clothes and houses me. *I* in the midst of me is not limited. *I* in the midst of me has always provided everything. *I* in the midst of me dwells secretly, hidden from view, sacred and silent. *I* has been given a human identity to hide behind. My human identity is only a mask, but let me no longer be fooled by my own mask. *I, I, I, I* . . .

Dare to believe. Dare to say "I," and know that you are

speaking your true name. *"I" is the name of God.* That is *you;* that is really you. When the scriptures say, "For my name's sake," the true name's sake is the name of you, "I."

*I* is the invisible presence within you. *I* is the invisible presence that goes before you to make the way clear, is always with you as your protection if you call upon it and hear its voice. "Listen to ME, *I,* look unto ME, the *I* of your own being. Don't look to effects. Your body is only the temple of 'I'; *I* made it in my image and likeness, of my substance. *I* knew you before you were conceived in the womb. *I* formed your body.

"I am the way, live by Me. Do not live by the way of the world, do not live by form. *I* am your high tower. Put up your sword; don't live by the physical or the mental. Live by the recognition of *I* always with and as you. *I* in the midst of you is ordained. . . ."

I, LOVE, and YOU are all the same word. Your capacity to love is your capacity to experience the *I* of another. Supreme love is when you see another as your own *I,* when you see yourself in another because you have gone beyond form and know *I.* When you love another and see your *I* as his *I,* you have become *total:* all is one.

When you need rest, when you need help, pick up the Bible and read St. John; see how over and over Jesus said the password. You will be amazed at how many times he voiced the word in just a few of the latter chapters. But as you read it, translate it into the truth. Consciously know that every time he says "I," he means YOU. Each time feel your *I,* see your *I,* and know that it is the *only* truth of you. "I AM the good shepherd, and know my sheep, and am known of mine."

"I, if I be lifted up, will draw all men unto me." Lift up your own "I," lift it up. Dare to know, dare to feel, dare to believe.

"I came not to judge the world, but to save the world. . . . I have not spoken of myself but of the Father which sent me. . . . Let not your heart be troubled: he that believeth in God believeth also in me, *I.* . . . In my Father's house are many mansions. . . ." Many, many, many different expressions of *I.* "If it were not so, I would have told you." If it were not so, your own *I* would not have led you into this meditation. And "I go to prepare a place for you. . . . I will come again and receive you unto myself, that where I AM there may ye be." "I am the way, the truth, and the life: no man cometh unto the Father, but by me." By *I*. "I AM in the Father and the Father in me. . . . I will not leave you comfortless: I will come to you. . . . Because I live, ye shall live also. At that day ye shall know that I AM in my Father, and ye in me, and I in you. . . . My peace I give unto you." You have not earned it, it IS you—a gift of yourself.

Now we have arrived. "Now you are clean through the word which I have spoken unto you. Abide in me and I in you. The branch cannot bear fruit itself, except it abide in the vine. For I am the vine, and he that abideth in me and I in him beareth much fruit." There is no other God than *I*.

The search for the Holy Grail has been our search for the whole man embodied in perfect idea, *I*. We have gone to churches to search for the Grail. We have sought gurus. Our search has been our drinking of the cup of becoming. Now, at last, we have surrendered. That means we have come home and stopped trying to find out who we are. We have given up. And, by surrendering, we have found that the Holy Grail has been with us always, that we need not have roamed the world of material sense to find it, that it has always been at our own home, for the Holy Grail is *I*. Our search is over, for we have found *I* within us.

The Holy Grail is the fourth dimension, it is grace, it is allness, it is *I*.

And now, one final clue: Beyond surrender is SILENCE. Beyond thought or struggle is *silence*. Our meditation is complete when there is no more thought, when we sit in the *silence*. Silence is love. In silence and in peace.

*I AM IN SILENCE*

Those who wish to communicate with the author or to receive information about recordings, lectures and publications direct your correspondence to Walter Starcke, Guadalupe Press, Box 865, Boerne, Texas, 78006